CORPORATE ETHICS AND CRIME

CORPORATE ETHICS AND CRIME

THE ROLE OF MIDDLE MANAGEMENT

Marshall B. Clinard

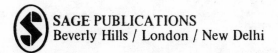

SAGE PUBLICATIONS
Beverly Hills / London / New Delhi

This document is the result of research supported by Grant Number 81-IJ-CX-0035 awarded by the National Institute of Justice, U.S. Department of Justice under the Justice System Improvement Act of 1979. Points of view or opinions stated in this document are those of the author and do not necessarily represent the official position or policies of the U.S. Department of Justice.

For information address:

SAGE Publications, Inc.
275 South Beverly Drive
Beverly Hills, California 90212

SAGE Publications India Pvt. Ltd.
C-236 Defence Colony
New Delhi 110 024, India

SAGE Publications Ltd
28 Banner Street
London EC1Y 8QE, England

Printed in the United States of America

Library of Congress Cataloging in Publication Data

Clinard, Marshall Barron, 1911-
　　Corporate ethics and crime.

　　Bibliography: p.
　　1. White collar crimes—United States.
2. Corporations—United States—Corrupt practices.
3. Industrial management—United States—Moral
and ethical aspects.　I. Title.
HV6769.C562　1983　　364.1'68'0973　　83-3105
ISBN 0-8039-1972-7

FIRST PRINTING

CONTENTS

Preface 7
1. White Collar and Corporate Crime 9
2. Middle Management 21
3. Ethics of Industry and Corporations 35
4. Why Some Corporations Are More Ethical than Others 53
5. The Role of Top Management 71
6. Pressures on Middle Management 91
7. Government Regulation 103
8. Interpretation 131
Appendix A 165
Appendix B 171
Appendix C 173
Bibliography 177
Index 183
About the Author 189

PREFACE

Within recent years the public, congressional committees, many business executives, and others have been concerned about the extent of unethical and illegal practices within the corporate world. At the same time, there is a recognition that many large corporations maintain consistently good records of ethical practices and compliance with the law that contrast sharply with the behavior of other corporations. The underlying reasons for these differences thus present several important issues.

Middle management may well be the most useful source for answering these and related questions. It is these executives who are responsible for carrying out top management's directives in the areas of procurement, manufacturing, and marketing. Within the organizational structure of any large corporation they are the focal point between top management and the supervisory staff. They have personally seen how pressures within a large corporation may contribute to unethical or illegal behavior.

This book is unique in the sense that, for the first time, views are presented about middle management's opinions regarding corporate ethical, unethical, or illegal behavior. What middle management has to say about these matters should increase our understanding of the processes within large corporations that account for them. In this study lengthy interviews were conducted with a considerable number of retired Fortune 500 middle management executives whose average service with their corporations covered a third of a century. The interviews focused on the validity of the following issues:

- Why some corporations are more ethical than are others.
- The extent to which top management sets the policies that lead either to ethical or unethical behavior or to compliance with, or violation of, the law.
- Whether undue corporate pressures on middle management may lead to the commission of illegal or unethical behavior.
- Whether some corporations are traditionally characterized by an ethical culture while others appear to be unethical, regardless of who is in top management.

- Whether corporate employers, particularly middle management, should report serious corporate violations to the government when top management has not acted on them.
- To what extent competitive practices lead to situations conducive to unethical practices or to law violations.
- Whether government regulation, as a whole, creates such a generally negative attitude toward government that it can lead to law violations.
- Whether industry self-regulation would be superior to government regulation.

In the concluding chapter, the findings in this study are analyzed in relation to the extent to which the views expressed by middle management coincide with the existing literature. An attempt has also been made to draw further implications from the statements of these executives that might lead to increased corporate ethical behavior and compliance with the law.

Several acknowledgments are in order. The study was supported by a grant from the National Institute of Justice, United States Department of Justice. In this connection, appreciation should also be expressed to Bernard Auchter, my liaison with the National Institute of Justice, for his critical assistance and his constant encouragement during the period of this difficult research. It should be emphasized, however, that the views expressed in this book are entirely mine and do not necessarily reflect those of the funding agency.

All interviews were conducted by myself, but Nancy Bell, a graduate student at the Anderson School of Business Management, University of New Mexico, was extremely helpful in preparing the material for computer analysis. The statistical analyses and computer programming were carried out efficiently by Judith Shontze. Donald J. Newman, Dean of the School of Criminal Justice, State University of New York — Albany, and Robert F. Meier, Professor of Sociology, Washington State University, read the original manuscript and made useful suggestions for its improvement. My wife, Ruth Blackburn Clinard, was, as with my previous books, an essential ingredient through her suggestions, editing, and continuous interest in the project. Finally, I should like to acknowledge the generosity of all the middle management executives who agreed to be interviewed and who put their trust in me as to the confidentiality of the interviews, which has obviously precluded by naming them. My indebtedness to each of them is profound; I found them to be persons who are a credit to the corporate world.

– Marshall B. Clinard
Santa Fe, New Mexico

1

*W*HITE *C*OLLAR AND
*C*ORPORATE *C*RIME

This study examines how a number of retired Fortune 500 middle management executives view the ethics and illegal behavior of large corporations, as well as their own roles. Dealing as it does with both ethics and corporate law violations, the study falls within the general area of white collar crime, since what began as unethical business practices have frequently become illegal behavior.

White collar crime includes corporate crime. These crimes constitute a large body of violations that are not normally associated with such ordinary crimes as burglary, larceny, robbery, assault, and so forth. They differ in the nature of the offense and the situations in which they occur, and the penalties imposed are far more likely to be administrative and civil rather than criminal in nature, even where a criminal penalty is available. A broader legal coverage of white collar crime is necessary, for without it many white collar violations (as, for example, the illegal acts committed by doctors or other professionals whose licenses may be revoked for serious offenses) cannot be regarded within the same context as ordinary crimes subject to criminal law. Although white collar offenses generally involve illegal financial acts, they may also be associated with actual or potential injury, or even death. Pharmacists, for example, may dispense barbiturates and similar drugs without a legal prescription, and corporations may violate safety regulations designed to protect workers and consumers from serious injury or death. A number of alternative penalties are also provided by the law for these types of offenses.

Thus corporate crime, like white collar crime (of which it is a part), is defined here as any act punishable by the state, regardless of whether it is punished by administrative or civil law, which it usually is, or under the criminal law. More specifically, corporate crime has been defined as the "conduct of a corporation, or individuals acting on behalf of the corporation, that is proscribed by law" (Braithwaite, 1982: 1466). This broad legal definition of corporate crime is important and necessary, since a corporation cannot be jailed, though it can be fined and its officers imprisoned. The major penalty of imprisonment provided for ordinary offenders is not available for cases involving corporations per se. For the most part, these offenses are handled by quasi-judicial bodies, including government regulatory agencies like the Food and Drug Administration. The law generally provides these agencies with *alternative* administrative, civil, or criminal actions, although some agencies do not provide for any criminal penalties. Furthermore, the difficulties encountered, the lengthy procedures of most court actions, as well as the necessity to take prompt action, make it expedient for many agencies to rely heavily on administrative penalties, such as the seizure or recall of commodities, consent agreements not to repeat the violation, and monetary penalties. The latter, for example, are often used by the Internal Revenue Service in income tax cases. Under civil law, wide use is made of consent decrees, injunctions, and civil monetary penalties. It is generally impossible to determine the seriousness of a corporate offense by the nature of the action taken. A major study of violations of corporate law by the Fortune 500 found that even serious violations generally receive only administrative sanctions; in fact, two-thirds of the serious cases and four-fifths of the moderately serious were handled in this manner (Clinard and Yeager, 1980: 124).

The work of Edwin H. Sutherland provided the impetus for basic changes in both the concept of and legal approaches to corporate offenses. In legal terms, business and corporate offenders are "administratively segregated" from ordinary crime, not because of what they do, but because of differences in the legal terminology (Sutherland, 1949: 8). On the whole, laws that affect corporations are fairly new, and the economic and political powers of the corporate world have been marshaled to discourage or prevent the application of criminal penalties to violations of corporate law and thus to avoid the approbrium of the terms "crime" and "criminal." Unless a more inclusive legal definition of crime is used, it is not possible to consider corporate law violations within the same framework as ordinary crime.

Criminologists began to develop an interest in white collar, and particularly corporate, crime only after Sutherland gave his presidential address to the American Sociological Society in 1939. Following the publication of his paper, in which he coined the term "white collar criminality," Sutherland did extensive research on the violations committed by seventy of the largest nonfinancial U.S. corporations, a report of which was published in 1949 as *White-Collar Crime*. In this book, Sutherland extended the definition of crime beyond the criminal law to include acts punishable by administrative and civil law. In the Foreword to the 1961 edition of the book, Cressey wrote: "The lasting merit of this book . . . is its demonstration that a pattern of crime can be found to exist outside both the focus of popular preoccupation with crime and the focus of scientific investigation of crime and criminality" (Cressey, 1961: xii). There followed research by Clinard (1952), Cressey (1953), Lane (1953/1977), Hartung (1950/1977), Quinney (1963/1977), and Newman (1953), as well as several important theoretical works by Aubert (1952/1977), Quinney (1964/1977), and Newman (1958/1977). One writer has referred to the period from 1940 to 1960 as the "classic period" of theory and research on white collar crime (Vaughan, 1981: 135). This two-decade period was followed by another decade of criminological research, most of which was concentrated almost exclusively on ordinary crime. A significant reason for this lack of interest in white collar and corporate crime was reflected in the conclusions presented in a theoretical article by Quinney (1963/1977: 292).

> Although there has been considerable interest and activity in the study of white-collar crime, the development of the area has been hampered by a number of problems that have not been made explicit. The concept has remained unclear because criminologists have subsumed different behavior under the term. In addition, writers have varied on the amount of emphasis given to the social status of the offender, have employed different meanings of

occupational activity, and have lacked consistency in designating the illegal nature of the offense.

It was not until the early 1970s that serious interest again developed in the area of white collar crime, especially corporate crime. This was due in part to a number of forces, including the growing consumer movement. During this period, much research was done on a wide variety of individual white collar occupational offenses, victims of white collar crime, and on the criminal justice aspects of white collar crime, including prosecution and sentencing. This concentration on the individual white collar offender has been typical of criminological research in the past, and for the most part it remains so today. An individualistic approach, however, does not work well when one is trying to explain the illegal behavior of an organization such as a large corporation. It became necessary, therefore, in order to understand white collar, and particularly corporate, illegal behavior, to create a macrolevel approach to the understanding of a macrolevel phenomenon; in other words, to study the social structure of organizations rather than primarily individuals, as in the case of ordinary crime (Vaughan, 1981: 137-138). Such an approach began to develop in the late 1970s, although it had an important beginning in a paper presented in 1966 by Reiss (1978: 35-36). Here he developed the concept of "organizational deviance," in which deviant behavior is to be explained largely through "the study of social organization — the organizational matrix that encompasses the deviant behavior of persons and the deviant behavior of organizations . . . Indeed the theory of organizations can be easily adapted to the study of organizational deviance."

OCCUPATIONAL VERSUS ORGANIZATIONAL CRIME

White collar crime may be occupational, or it may be organizational. The former consists of violations committed by individuals or small groups in connection with their occupations (see Clinard and Quinney, 1973: 187-205), including violations by persons in such legitimate occupations as physicians, pharmacists, lawyers, auto or appliance repairmen, bank tellers, and small businessmen. Occupational crimes by persons in business include the following: tax evasion; embezzlement; illegal manipulations in the retail sale of used cars and other products; fraudulent repairs of automobiles, television sets, and appliances; check-kiting; and violations in the sales of securities. Some government employees and politicians commit a number of occupational offenses such as the direct misappropriation of public funds or the illegal acquisition of these funds through padded payrolls, the illegal placement of relatives on their payrolls, or the acceptance of monetary payments from appointees. They may also gain financially by giving favors to business firms; for example, they may issue fraudulent licenses or certificates, or they might lower tax evaluations or give tax exemptions illegally. Physicians may prescribe narcotics illegally, perform illegal abortions, make fraudulent reports or give false testimony in accident cases, or they may split fees. Illegal activities among lawyers include the misappropriation of funds in receiverships, abetting perjured testimony from witnesses, and various forms of "ambulance chasing." Members of most other occupations may also violate the law in a wide variety of ways.

Organizational crime is a distinct form of white collar crime. Gross (1978: 56) defines organizations as groups that "coordinate efforts toward the attainment of collective goals," such as large corporations and labor unions. He has pointed out that "our ability to understand, let alone control, organizational crime requires going beyond theories of individual deterrence and punishment. We shall have to study organizations themselves and the organizational world they have created" (Gross, 1980: 73). Therefore, one cannot explain organizational crime without looking at the organization in question as a social system. With this in mind, an attempt was made by Finney and Lesieur (1982) to construct a contingency theory, or a model for organizational crime. They concluded that the "essential components in its development were a recognition that organizations as well as individuals commit crimes to achieve their objectives and solve their problems and that commitment to deviant courses of action involves normal processes of decision making under conditions of limited rationality" (Finney and Lesieur, 1982: 289).[1]

The focus on goals is the central characteristic of organizations and, therefore, of organizational crime; in fact, organizations are evaluated in terms of their successes or failures in the attainment of goals. To be successful, each organization must have an internal social structure designed to achieve its goals, consisting of internal processes and hierarchical series of positions or status relationships. Organizations vary in the ways in which their social structures systematically and continuously generate unlawful organizational behavior. Of considerable importance is the fact that some internal social structures and processes "often tend to produce tension for organizations to obtain goals unlawfully" (Vaughan, 1982: 1378).

Individual members in a large organization generally become linked to the organization's successes and future goals. Since the interests of the members and the organization coincide, employees may engage in behavior that is unethical or unlawful, "using the skills, knowledge and resources associated with their position to do so" (Vaughan, 1982: 1391). Thus, organizational crime occurs as part of working on behalf of an organization to achieve its goals; it takes place in the course of work by those who participate in the organization (Finney and Lesieur, 1982: 264).

CORPORATE CRIME

During the twentieth century, astounding growth has been occurring in multinational corporations. These giants produce the bulk of all manufactured products, dominate much of the world's economy in their global operations, employ millions of workers, and exercise a major influence on consumer choices. Their vast and varied financial resources have enabled them to adopt, as well as to change, technology on a massive scale. By this means they have brought enormous industrial and commercial progress to the entire Western world and, increasingly, to the developing world.

Along with the large corporations' greatly increased productive power, an equally significant potential for social harm and a lack of social responsibility has evolved (Bradshaw and Vogel, 1981). There has been evidence of extensive violations of the law. These have been widely revealed in many governemnt investigative committees, both state and federal, that have looked into banking institutions, stock exchange operations, railroads, and the large oil, food, and drug industries, among others. Investigations have also exposed widespread corporate payoffs (domestic and foreign) and illegal political contributions. All of these investigations have revealed the immense economic and political power of corporations.

Nearly two-thirds of the Fortune 500 corporations were charged with violations of corporate law over a two-year period (1975-1976); one-half of these were charged with a serious or a moderately serious violation (Clinard and Yeager, 1980: 113, 118). At least one sanction was imposed on 321 of the corporations (Clinard and Yeager, 1980: 122). Using imposed court sanctions, one study found that 11 percent of the Fortune 500 were involved in a major law violation between 1970 and 1979 (Ross, 1980: 57). A more recent study found that 115 corporations of the Fortune 500 had been convicted between 1970 and 1980 of at least one major crime or had paid civil penalties for serious illegal behavior (U.S. News and World Report, 1982: 25-26). Allowing for size, the largest of the Fortune 500 corporations have been found to be the chief violators (Clinard and Yeager, 1980: 119). Moreover, they have received a widely disproportionate share of the sanctions for serious and moderate violations.

These corporate violations have resulted in enormous economic losses to consumers and the government (Ross, 1980). Such illegal practices include pricefixing, false advertising claims, the marketing of unsafe products, environmental pollution, political bribery, foreign payoffs, disregard of safety regulations in manufacturing cars and other products, the evasion of taxes, and the falsification of corporate records to hide illicit practices. There have also been injuries (and even deaths) among citizens and employees because of unsafe drugs and other products, pollution, and unprotected work conditions. Such serious illegal acts, knowingly committed against consumers, their own workers, their competitors, and even against foreign nations, have often involved tremendous sums of money.

Public opinion polls have shown an increasing lack of confidence in corporate business, largely because of unethical and illegal corporate behavior, as well as an accompanying lack of social responsibility. Harris polls showed a drop in confidence in the heads of large corporations from 55 percent in 1965 to 21 percent in 1974, and to 15 percent in 1975. In fact, the 1975 poll found that 80 percent of the American people believed that "if left alone, big business would be greedy, selfish, make inordinate profits at the expense of the public," and that "if left un-checked, big business would stifle competition." A 1975 Gallup poll found that, among all institutions comprising "the United States power structure," big business came in last, with a "confidence" score of only 34 percent. A study by Lipset and Schneider (1978) concluded that business had dropped in public esteem during the previous decade — not only business overall, but specific industries and major corporations. Various other surveys have found widely held opinions by the public that prices and profits are often excessively high, product quality unreliable, and corporate interest in the well-being of individual citizens minimal (The Wall Street Journal, August 31, 1978).

On the other hand, a sizable proportion of these large corporations maintain high ethical standards and exhibit significant social responsi-bility in their dealings with the public, consumers, and workers. A two-year study (1975-1976) found that 40 percent of the Fortune 500 corporations had not been charged with any violations of law by any of the 25 federal agencies during that period of time (Clinard and Yeager, 1980: 113).[2] The problem of why some corporations are charged with violations and other are not, and why some have strong ethical stan-dards while others are frequently unethical, is an important one that will be examined later in this study (see Chapter 4).

Today, the public regards white collar and corporate crime as serious offenses. A 1978 national survey in which 204 offenses were ranked for seriousness revealed, for example, that the public considers such offenses equal to, and even more serious than, many "ordinary crimes such as burglary and robbery" (Wolfgang, 1979). An even more recent study has shown that during the past decade, white collar and corporate offenses have generally been perceived by the public to be even more serious than in the past (Cullen et al., 1982). Particularly stronger than in the past are attitudes toward corporate offenses that have resulted in death or injury (for example, defective autos) and toward pricefixing by corporations.

The increased recognition of illegal corporate behavior within re-cent years by professional criminologists and others has been a natural response to various identifiable social forces, and particularly to the dramatic increase in the impact of the major corporations on American society in general. Some of these forces include, for example, the effects of Watergate, some highly publicized corporate violations, the increased recognition of extensive corporate irresponsibility,[3] the growth of the consumer movement, a growing concern for the environment, and an awareness of the overconcentration of public and governmental concern on crimes among the lower classes (Clinard and Yeager, 1979). In spite of this greatly increased interest in corporate crime since Sutherland's pioneering work, however, there has been only one similarly comprehensive research study (Clinard et al., 1979; Clinard and Yeager, 1980).

CORPORATE CRIME AS ORGANIZATIONAL BEHAVIOR

The immensity, the diffusion of responsibility, and the heirarchical structure of large corporations all foster conditions conducive to organizational deviance. In addition, the nature of corporate goals may promote unethical and illegal behavior. For these reasons, corporate illegalities must be viewed as organizational behavior. Using this orientation, organizational theory can provide valuable insights into how the unique nature of corporations as large-scale organizations relates to the unethical and illegal behavior that does occur (Reiss, 1978; Gross, 1978). In contrast to ordinary crime or white collar occupational crime, corporate crime is committed by organizations or by "collectivities of discrete individuals; it is hardly comparable to the actions of a lone individual" (Shapiro, 1976: 14). Although the law treats corporations as tangible "persons," illegal corporate behavior cannot be explained, nor even adequately explored, within the framework of those theories of deviance and crime that are applied to individuals involved in ordinary (and most occupational) crime.

Illegal corporate behavior is a form of collective rule-breaking in order to achieve the organizational goals (Sherman, 1980: 4-5). Viewed in this manner, corporate crime results from the behavior of groups of persons organized in a common purpose (Meier, 1975), and from the linkage of individuals and groups within the organization to achieve corporate goals (Shover, 1978: 39). Hence, the achievement of objectives is crucial to a definition of corporate crime as "the illegal acts of omission or commission of an individual or group of individuals in a legitimate formal organization in accordance with the operational goals of the organization" (Shrager and Short, 1978).

In the case of some organizations where goals may generate crimes, the goal emphasis may be reduced or modified. In the case of large corporations, however, this is difficult to do, for their primary goal is to maximize profits for the stockholders and, simultaneously and indirectly, for top management. Although large corporations may have other goals, such as the increase of maintenance of corporate power and prestige, along with corporate growth and stability, their paramount objectives are the maximization of profits and the general financial success of the corporation, whether through sales, market shares, or increased assets. "No matter how strongly managers prefer to pursue other objectives and no matter how difficult it is to find profit-maximizing strategies in a world of uncertainty and high information costs, failure to satisfy this criterion means ultimately that a firm will disappear from the economic scene" (Scherer, 1980: 38). One might expect that under these conditions, a corporation is most likely to engage in unlawful conduct when support diminishes for legitimate procedures to be used in reaching the profit goal. Under these conditions, firms may violate anti-trust laws and the regulations of the FTC, OSHA, EPA, and other agencies if, by complying, the costs to the corporation will be too high.

As in all large organizations, the achievement of corporate goals is accomplished within a complex hierarchical context of social relationships and expectations. This system of relative power and status among various individuals can also lead to unethical practices or illegal behavior on the part of a corporation. In large corporations, the social structure consists, on the one hand, of those with much power — the board of directors, top executives like the chairmen of the board, the presidents, the chief executive officers, and the vice-presidents — while on the other side are those with less power — the middle managers, the supervisors, and the workers. The differing aspirations and pressures within this hierarchy can be conducive to unethical or illegal behavior at a number of levels. At the same time, the continuing relationships between the parent corporation and its subsidiaries may be crime-generating due to the great pressures to show profits.

In this research we will examine, through the eyes of middle management, how the structural relationships and pressures in a large corporation contribute to unethical and illegal behavior or, in some cases, to ethical behavior and compliance with government laws and regulations. We shall examine factors that operate internally, some that might well contribute to these situations, as well as external factors impinging on the corporation.

NOTES

1. Other factors in their organizational model include "the conduciveness of the surrounding culture, internal and external sources of performance pressure, internal and external controls, and the complex of societal reactions to organizational crime and of the offending enterprises' reactions to these reactions that recursively affect the likelihood of yet further violations" (Finney and Lesieur, 1982: 289).

2. This does not mean, however, that all of these corporations were necessarily "clean." Some simply might not have been caught, particular industries might not have been well policed, or their corporate counsels might have been more successful in preventing violations or in preventing the lodging of formal charges, because of greater familiarity with the law.

3. In a 1981 Gallup poll, the public ranked business executives fifteenth in honesty and ethical standards in a list of occupations.

2

MIDDLE MANAGEMENT

There are two types of middle managers: the traditional type, who "command" people, and the newer type, who dispense technical and professional knowledge. The latter include, for example, geologists, research scientists, corporate planners, and system designers, none of whom have control over many personnel (Drucker, 1976: 477-478). Traditionally, middle managers "manage" other managers and supervisors, appearing on corporate organizational charts under titles such as manager, assembly operations; manager, regional sales; and plant manager. Middle management's position in any individual corporation is a crucial one, for on their decisions rests the actual carrying out of top management's directives. The effectiveness of their role seriously affects procurement, manufacturing, marketing, and all other areas of corporate activity. Their important and vulnerable position has been associated with their serving as the focal point in a well-balanced organizational relationship between senior management, junior management, and their middle management colleagues (Morris, 1975). One factor is clear: They appear to be subjected to excessive pressures, while at the same time their role in decision making and in the delegation of responsibility is often not sufficiently recognized by top management. Their positions have often made them the "oppressed middle," a phrase used as the title of a recent book, consisting primarily of case studies, that delineates the problems faced by middle management executives (Shorris, 1980).

THE ISSUES

This research on middle management deals with its views of the varied internal and external factors that operate to produce unethical or illegal behavior within a corporation. The interest in these internal factors stems from the structural hierarchy of a corporation and its relationship to corporate violations. The following internal factors are considered: (1) the role that top management plays in unethical practices and illegal behavior, (2) the role of the excessive pressures exerted by top management on middle management, (3) the extent to which corporations are characterized by unethical or ethical cultures, and (4) the degree to which the nature of corporate organization precludes employee cooperation with government in dealing with corporate violations. Viewed externally, the concern is with (1) the role of competitive practices and (2) the influence of generally negative attitudes produced by government regulations.

Relatively few studies have been conducted in the area of corporate ethics and law violations, and most have used statistics, case material, and economic data, or they have analyzed legal issues. This study is unique in two ways; it approaches corporate ethics and violations from an individual, social psychological perspective, and for the first time it examines this issue, as well as the social structure of a corporation and its status hierarchy, through the eyes of middle management.[1] Questionnaires were not used; instead, lengthy interviews were conducted with retired middle management executives about their views in regard to corporate ethics, illegal behavior, and the most important factors involved.[2] The research focused on the validity of the following statements:

Top management, particularly the chief executive officer, sets the policies that lead either to ethical or unethical behavior or to compliance with, or violation of, the law by the corporation. The policies set by top management greatly affect the behavior of middle management. Moreover, top management is generally aware of the more important types of violations that occur within a corporation.

Undue corporate pressures upon middle management may lead to their becoming engaged in illegal or unethical behavior. Middle management often receives directives from top management regarding desired goals, whether of production or sales quotas, the development of new products, or other areas. These goals can be perceived as absolute demands that may require, and even appear to justify, any means to fulfill them.

Certain corporations are traditionally characterized by an ethical culture, while others appear to be unethical regardless of top management personnel. Corporations generally tend to be characterized by a culture that includes goals: corporate "heroes," as in the case of corporate founders and others; the corporate image presented to the world; and even the manner in which employees are directed to dress and behave (Deal and Kennedy, 1982; Olins, 1978). A recent study of the best-run large American corporations found them to be characterized by a distinctive, eight-trait "internal cultural pattern" that is notably missing from weaker large corporations (Peters and Waterman, 1982). The culture concept is extended one step further in this study to include differences in corporate ethics and compliance with the law. In fact, Stone (1975) has referred to the "culture of a corporation" as an entire constellation of attitudes and forces, some of which contribute to illegal behavior. Some corporations appear to become permeated with their own particular standards in relation to law obedience and overall good citizenship. A recent study of the Fortune 500 found, for example, that a small percentage of violating corporations committed a highly disproportionate share of all infractions cited (Clinard and Yeager, 1980: 116-117). Only 38 of the 300 manufacturing corporations cited for violations during 1975 and 1976, or 13 percent (8 percent of all corporations studied), accounted for 52 percent of all violations — an average of 23.5 per firm. Disproportionate percentages were also found for environmental, manufacturing, administrative, and labor violations, although not for financial and trade infractions.

Corporate employees, particularly middle management, will not, because of corporate loyalties, report serious corporate violations to the government, even though they had been reported to the highest corporate level.

Competitive practices lead to situations conducive to unethical corporate practices or to law violations. The unethical or illegal practices of competitors in the same line of business virtually force a corporation to adopt these practices in order to show financial profits.

Government regulation, as a whole, creates such a generally negative attitude toward government that it tends to lead to violations. Self-regulation by industry would be superior to government regulation.

THE SAMPLE

The research sample consisted of 64 retired middle management executives who had been employed by corporations listed in the Fortune 500 during the past five years.[3] All Fortune 500 corporations are in industrial production (manufacturing and mining) and exclude retail and wholesale outlets, banks, insurance companies, and utilities. The average length of the executives' employment with a single corporation was 31.8 years; three-fourths of them had never worked for another corporation.

Certain sample criteria were set: Each executive must have been retired ten years or less and must have been in an actual management position — procurement, manufacturing, marketing, financial/accounting, or similar areas. Excluded were executives in such individually specialized professional work as geologists for oil corporations or research scientists for pharmaceutical corporations, as well as persons whose duties had been in plant maintenance or similar nonproduct responsibilities. Interviews were obtained from the following areas: Santa Fe, New Mexico (where the researcher resides), Phoenix, and most (87.5 percent) from the retirement communities of Sun City and Green Valley, Arizona. Sun City, a retirement community of 58,000 persons, is situated in the Phoenix suburbs, and Green Valley, a community of 16,000 retirees, is south of Tucson. The procedures and problems involved in locating the sample are described in Appendix A.

The selection of retired executives was based on a number of premises. First, since retired executives generally have more free time, there would be no pressures from time limitations such as might be experienced with presently employed executives. Under such conditions, a more lengthy interview about corporate life could be conducted. Second, it was assumed that retired executives would talk more freely about corporate operations and pressures on middle management than they would if currently employed. Third, their retirement status might also mean that they would like to have the opportunity to talk candidly, and to reminisce, about past corporate happenings, though in a typical retirement community it is generally not the practice to talk in great detail about who one has been and what one has done.

The executives interviewed had been retired ten years or less. Originally, the limit had been set at no more than five years, but this period was soon found to be impractical if one were to obtain a sufficient sample of executives, as most of them had been retired for more than five years. Many executives tend to spend one to three years after retirement either in their home communities or in various retirement areas while trying to decide on a permanent retirement community. The mean length of retirement for the sample was 6.5 years, the median 6.2. About half (53.1 percent) had been retired six years or less, and 46.9 percent between six and ten years. Two had been retired one year, and seven for two. One of the best interviews was with an executive who had been retired for ten years; he was extremely verbal, had a good memory, and furnished many useful comments. In general, the only research questions likely to be affected by the length of retirement would be those dealing with newer government regulations. However, most of the retirees read *The Wall Street Journal* and thus keep up with the situation regarding regulations in an overall way. Of a sample of thirty interviewees, nineteen read this newspaper regularly, ten occasionally, and only one not at all. Memory for older events, such as what went on during their years with the corporations, probably does not decline a great deal anyway.

CHARACTERISTICS OF THE SAMPLE

Due to the problems encountered in locating a sample (see Appendix A), no valid claim can be be made that the sample is representative of the Fortune 500 middle management. Certainly it was not obtained through the usually recognized methods of random sampling. On the other hand, no known bias is present; in fact, chance operated throughout the selective process. Actually, it turned out to resemble a "stratified sample," in that it had wide distribution, whether the number of corporations (51), their size, the type of industry, the executive's position in the corporation, age, length of retirement, or education were being considered. On the whole, the answers revealed a great variety of responses. Through a comparison with data from other sources, it was also discovered that there was a good spread of corporations that tended to violate the law and of those that did not.

Distribution and Size of Corporation

The sample came from 51 Fortune 500 corporations (see Appendix B). Although it had been hoped that it would be possible to have a corporation represented by only one interviewee, this was made impossible by the difficulties encountered in locating middle management persons who met the other sample criteria. In the end, 41 corporations were represented by one person, seven by two people, and three by three. Fortunately, where there were multiple representatives of a corporation, the individuals were seldom involved in the same corporate function, such as procurement, manufacturing, marketing, or finance/accounting. Even where this did occur, their responses to the questions were not necessarily similar.

According to the Fortune 500 ranking by sales, from which the sample came, greater variation was found in the size of the corporations than had originally been anticipated. It had been thought that they would be biased, in that the largest fifty corporations would constitute nearly all of the sample, whereas they actually constituted only half (47.5 percent). Persons from corporations that ranked 51-100 in size totaled 15 (24.6 percent), those from 101-200, 18.0 percent, and those 201 or over, 9.8 percent. Three corporations were not included in these figures because in 1980 they were no longer listed among the Fortune 500.

Types of Industry

A wide range of industries was represented in the sample. Grouped into the following categories, largely following Fortune 500 classification, the distribution was:

Motor Vehicles	12
Industrial and Farm Equipment	9
Metal Manufacturing and Metal Products	8
Chemicals	8
Electric and Appliances	5
Oil Refining and Petroleum Products	5
Food Processing and Beverages	5
Drugs and Cosmetics	4
Other	4

Length of Service

Generally, the executives had been with their last corporation for an extremely long period of time. The length of time ranged from 8 to 45 years, with a mean of 31.8 and a median of 34.8. Two-thirds (64.1

percent) had been with a corporation from 31 to 45 years. Three-fourths of them had never worked for any other Fortune 500 corporation, 21.9 percent had worked for one other Fortune 500 corporation, and only two had worked with two others.

Last Position

Executives were classified according to their last positions within the corporation (Appendix C gives their positions and titles). With few exceptions, this position followed the pattern of their previous five positions with the corporation. Marketing positions of various types represented the largest group (25, or 39.1 percent). Positions ranged from district sales manager and regional sales manager to divisional sales manager and general manager of marketing. Four executives' last positions were in foreign marketing.

The second largest category was manufacturing, with a percentage of 33.8. Four were plant or factory managers, and nearly all of the remainder were employed in various capacities at the divisional level or the home office.

Five retirees had last been employed in finance or accounting management, positions that also closely followed their previous posts. Their positions ranged from divisional cost accountant, to director of corporate taxes, to assistant treasurer.

The other category of thirteen interviewees was larger than one would like, but the positions were of such a wide range that it was difficult to make categories. All of them had been in management positions. Among the different types of work were research adminis-tration, labor relations, employee benefits, design engineering, and public relations. Unfortunately, only one executive was in procurement, which originally had been set up as a separate category. Executives in other areas spoke of unethical pressures on those in the procurement field and the possibility of their receiving kickbacks in purchasing arrangements. It would have been useful to have had sufficient persons from this area in order to reach some conclusions as to the validity of these assertions.

Location of Last Position

The majority (53.1 percent) of the executives in their last positions had been located in the home office of the corporation, and 20.3 percent in divisions there. Located in branch areas were 39.0 percent of the total; only five were working in a subsidiary. The small number of subsidiaries made it impossible to examine whether pressures to show results tend to be greater on the management of subsidiaries than on divisional management.

Age

The interviewees' ages ranged from 55 to 83, with a mean of 67.8 and a median of 67.4. In the 55-65 age group there were 26.6 percent; 66-70 was the largest group (43.8 percent); and 29.7 percent fell in the 71-83 age group. Generally, middle management executives retire around the age of 62-65; several in the lower age brackets had taken early retirement. The oldest executive, who was 83, had been retained by his corporation more than ten years beyond normal retirement; he was head of public relations, and from his sharpness and vigor one could readily see why the corporation thought his continued employment was needed. With regard to the success of the interviews, in terms of verbal response or the usefulness of their comments, the age of the interviewee did not appear to be a significant factor.

Length of Time Retired

This issue has already been discussed. To repeat, the sample was limited to those retired ten years or less. The range was from one to ten, the mean was 6.4, and the median 6.5. Length of retirement made no statistically significant difference on a test of eight variables.

Education

Educational background was recorded for 52 of the executives. A surprisingly high proportion, one out of four (28.8 percent), were not college graduates; 11.5 percent were high school graduates, while 17.3 percent had had some college education. Half of them had a college degree (only two were MBAs), and nine had had other graduate work. Many had taken special seminars that were either held by the corporations or by the industry, often on a university campus. Executives without college degrees did not view their treatment by the corporation as significantly different from that of those who had degrees. In fact, the lowest percentage of those who ranked their treatment as only "fair" were those with only a high school diploma.

THE INTERVIEWS

An interview schedule was constructed for the purpose of making the interviews as uniform as possible, and was then revised after a pretest that involved four interviews.[4] As a result of the pretest, it was discovered that several interviewees had been irritated by the repeated use of terminology such as "unethical" and "violations" in the wording of questions; some felt that these terms prejudged the corporate situation. As a result, the words "ethical" and "unethical" were substituted in order to project a more neutral stance, and the word "ethical" was frequently substituted for "violation" (although the definition of "ethics" given to the interviewees included "violations of law"). A few questions were dropped, particularly one that asked the interviewee's opinion of the extent of violations among corporations generally, as many of them said they could not answer this question. The questions relating to their own industries and corporations were retained, however.

The first page of the schedule consisted of "face sheet data" — information about the type of work they had done in the corporation, whether they had been in the home office or elsewhere, their age, education, length of retirement, number of years with the corporation, last position held, as well as the five previous positions held, attitudes about the treatment they had received from the corporation, whether they had ever been employed by another Fortune 500 corporation and, added later, how frequently they read *The Wall Street Journal*.

The final interview schedule consisted of eleven pages containing 27 questions, three of which had subparts. Fifteen questions had a scale answer (a five- or threeway gradation), and each was followed by a "Comment" as to the reasons for having chosen particular answers, or for any other remarks relevant to the question. Four questions required either "yes" or "no" answers, also with a comment. Eight questions were completely open-ended; these concerned individual views about a given issue.

The questions were devised to learn the opinions of middle management on various issues. Six questions had previously been asked of a small sample of top management executives (Clinard and Yeager, 1980). The questions were designed to ascertain interviewees' opinions of the ethical standards of their respective industries and corporations (ethics being defined as fairness and honesty to the public, consumers, competitors, and the government): why some corporations are unethical and violate the law, while others do not; whether corporations are basically unethical or ethical; their views about the extent of violations in their own corporations; the types of pressures on middle management and the effects these pressures have on unethical and illegal behavior, both generally and on themselves; the role of government regulations and which regulations they would like to see kept; whether industry can regulate itself; and the role of competitive practices in corporate law violations.

More peripheral questions were whether or not employees should report serious violations to the government if the corporation itself fails to correct them, whether top management should speak out against unethical and illegal behavior by corporations, and whether middle management resented the much greater salary and other compensation differentials between themselves and top management executives.

Retired middle management executives of the Fortune 500 have occupied important and significant positions in the American economy. It was assumed that in retirement they would generally exhibit a high degree of loyalty to the corporation (Rowan, 1981) on the basis of their long years of corporate service. Except for three individuals, none of the persons interviewed had ever met the researcher prior to the actual interview; he was simply the person who had telephoned them to ask to arrange an interview in which there had to be a great deal of trust on their part. In view of all these factors, the interview presented a potentially difficult situation in an effort to obtain reliable data.

All interviews were conducted in as identical a fashion as possible, with a standard explanation and interview schedule. A standard oral format was worked out to explain the study at the beginning of each interview, to reassure the interviewee of its confidentiality, and to clarify questions as the interview proceeded. Any personal comments by the interviewer were avoided if it was felt that they might bias the interview.

Interviews were carried out in a hotel room, with only a few exceptions. The original intention had been to interview the executives in their own homes, but in the pretest, and on the advice of others, it was concluded that this was not feasible. Home settings presented problems of assuring privacy throughout the interview, due to the presence of other persons, such as wives, or to such interruptions as telephone calls. It was also possible that a home visit might be regarded as an intrusion of the interviewees' privacy, which might lead to their declining to be interviewed, or the reverse could happen, should the interview be regarded as an opportunity for a social occasion. For this reason, all invitations to conduct the interview in a restaurant, as a guest of the interviewee, were declined.

An hour and a half was usually needed to complete the interview schedule. However, since the question period was always preceded by an approximate fifteen-minute "warm-up" to establish rapport, followed by a similar period at the termination of an interview, the total time required for each interview was two hours or slightly longer — sometimes up to three hours if a person was particularly verbal and gave numerous examples or anecdotes. During the "warm-up" period, there were usually such additional questions as to how long the person had been living in the area, if he had come directly from retirement, how he was enjoying the community, as well as retirement, his golf game, and other activities. Also, the respondent sometimes had further questions about the research project. The "termination" period covered conversation on various topics, including the interview, an expression of thanks for having granted the interview, and a request for assistance in obtaining the names of other possible interviewees.

From the outset of this project, it was recognized that it would be imperative to assure each interviewee of the complete confidentiality and anonymity of the interview. These executives, who had held high corporate positions, who would probably tend to be loyal to the corporation, and who might be concerned about their retirement pensions as well as other corporate benefits, were being asked their opinion regarding subjects that, to them, might be quite sensitive. It was therefore essential to establish a relationship of trust. If there was to be any withholding or falsifying of information, it should not be due to the fact that nothing had been done to avoid such a possibility. With this goal in mind, the following procedures were followed:

(1) The interviewer's former position as a professor at the University of Wisconsin Madison was emphasized, along with the fact that he had previously done a great deal of research of a completely confidential nature.

(2) Also emphasized was the fact that the researcher had previously held confidential interviews with several top management executives, all of which had remained completely confidential in subsequent publication of the research.

(3) When the interview schedule was shown to a respondent at the outset of the interview, it was pointed out that each schedule was being recorded only by code numbers, both for the individual executive and the name of the corporation involved. In this study, all comments are anonymous and no corporation is identified (a list of the corporations is given in Table A-1, Appendix A). All interviewees were assured that their names would never appear in any publication related to the research.

(4) With only one exception, no personal comments were ever made after any response to a question, with every effort being made to maintain a completely neutral reaction, including the control of facial expression. The one exception was when one respondent claimed that there is practically no pricefixing in the corporate world; only after the question was completed was a comment made with factual information that refuted this statement. Indeed, so neutral and noncommittal was the researcher's position that when one respondent said: "I have been talking at length now; what is your view of the questions?" the reply was: "My view is all the answers given by all of you."

(5) The comparable retirement status and age of the respondents and the researcher was of great help in establishing a milieu of confidence. In fact, the conclusion was reached that this interviewing could not have been successfully carried out by a younger person, and certainly not by one who was not a senior faculty member. Some of the interviewees so stated; when one of them was being assured, for example, about the anonymity of the interview responses, he replied: "I know you are a professional person."

On four or five occasions, even these factors did not allay all the suspicion encountered at the outset of the interview. Suspicion was manifested largely in respondents' asking for detailed information about the nature of the project, the use to which the information was to be put, the source of financial support, and so forth. In almost all of these cases, the researcher was able to reassure the interviewees with frankness and direct answers. Much to my continued amazement, inasmuch as few of them could have anticipated fully the wide scope and nature of the questions, no interview was terminated. Most of them said that they had found the questions stimulating.

At the beginning, it was thought that some hostility might be encountered, or even false answers given, were it known that the project was being supported by the government, particularly the U.S. Department of Justice. Some respondents might have become suspicious that their individual corporations were somehow being investigated; fortunately, this presented no problem whatsoever. At the outset of the telephone arrangements for the interviews, it was explained that a grant had been received for a study of middle management executives' opinions. Hardly any individuals asked about the source of the grant, indicating perhaps that businessmen know (or care) little about the mechanisms of research grant awards. To the few who did inquire further, the reply was given that it was a "government grant," and no more than four or five respondents asked further questions. When the exact source of the research grant was asked, no effort was made to answer other than frankly and fully. One may safely conclude, therefore, that the responses to the questions were not influenced by the source of the grant.

Based on a critical examination of the respondents' behavior during the interview, their statements that they had enjoyed it, letters received in which other names were suggested, and similar evidence, the conclusion appears to be justified that a genuine rapport had been established and that their answers were, on the whole, frank and honest. Every effort was made to probe further in order to bring out any possible negative aspects of the corporations being discussed. On the assumption that a highly positive personal view of their corporations might bias answers, two separate questions — one at the beginning, the other at the end — were inserted into the questionnaire in an effort to ascertain more specifically each individual's attitude toward his corporation: "Since retiring, what is your general feeling of how the corporation treated you?" and "What do you regard as the effects of pressures on your relations with the corporation?" Extreme personal loyalty to the corporation was expressed by such remarks as the following: "I am the kind of person who cherished the corporation, was proud of what I did, and I even brag today of their products. Some who worked for other corporations will not even buy their products."

Although three-fourths felt positive (only one-third felt very positive) about the general treatment they had received from their respective corporations, a substantial proportion of them, regardless of the degree of favorable treatment, expressed strong negative reactions to the work pressures to which they had been subjected and the excessive friction encountered in their relations with top management. Based on the answers to questions about their corporations, one might well conclude that in the final analysis, most of the respondents were not overly influenced by corporate loyalty.

NOTES

1. Studies have been made of top management's views of corporate ethics (see Silk and Vogel, 1976).
2. Silk and Vogel's (1976) study of the views of top management is the only other somewhat similar study, much of which dealt with business ethics and social responsibility. As part of their research, they were permitted to attend the closed meetings of the Conference Board, which consists of the top executives of the largest U.S. corporations; in their case, a total of 250 corporations were represented at various times. They included in their book an appraisal of the general discussion, as well as specific, anonymous quotes by top executives from 57 corporations. Their study made no use of statistical analyses, in contrast to this study.
3. The five-year period was necessary inasmuch as the corporations by which they had been employed might not now be listed in the Fortune 500, though they had been during the period of their employment. As it turned out, however, this applied to only three corporations.
4. The original intention had been to use a tape recorder, at least part of the time, but this was never done. In the pretests, a negative view toward any recorded statements was noted, and from later comments it was concluded that the use of any such device would have gravely affected the feeling of anonymity on the part of the respondents.

3

ETHICS OF INDUSTRY AND CORPORATIONS

EXECUTIVES' INDUSTRIES

"Business ethics" was defined for the executives as "fairness and honesty to the public, the consumer, competitors, and to the government." As thus defined, unethical business practices included violations of the law. Approximately two out of three executives approved of the ethics of their own industries: one-fourth (25.0 percent) regarded them as "very good," 43.8 percent as "good," and about one-third (31.3 percent) as "fair."

Respondents' views regarding the ethics within their own specific industries differed little in terms of the positions they had held within a corporation (manufacturing, marketing, finance, and other). For example, approximately one-fourth of the manufacturing and marketing personnel ranked their particular industries as "very good," and 47.6 percent and 40.0 percent, respectively, ranked their industries as "good." In this case, as in many others, chi-square tests of statistical significance were found to be invalid due to the small size of the sample, which affected the cell distribution (less than five cases per cell), and they are not reported. Length of retirement, however, was found to affect responses statistically when divided into two groups; those retired longer tended to have a more favorable view of their industries. The executives' highest proportional ratings for "very good" were, first, those in metals (metal manufacturing and metal products), and second, chemicals. The highest proportion who rated their industries as only "fair" were from the motor vehicle and aerospace industries. With a total of 64 cases split into 9 types of industry, however, the number in each analytical category was generally not large.

Respondents who expressed favorable views of their industry chiefly gave as their reasons, in order of frequency, that (1) there were few unethical practices, (2) their industries were better than others, (3) workers were treated fairly, and (4) larger corporations have better ethics than smaller ones.[1] Those who expressed a "fair" or less favorable opinion felt that there was too much industrial espionage, improper entertainment of prospective customers, pricefixing and other antitrust activity, both domestic and foreign payoffs, misrepresentation of products, and unsafe working conditions.

The high ethical standards reported for their own industries were frequently attributed to government regulations. Of particular importance was the continuing regulatory effect of pricefixing actions brought by the government, and several references were made to its salutary effect, even over a period of as long as fifty years when, for example, a court action was imposed. Considerable contradictions were noted, however, between the executives' general rating of their respective industries and the more specific comments that they made about them. The following comments were typical:

Very Good

I never heard anything about the industry that was detrimental. Corporations trade information with other corporations on safety and pollution problems. I never heard about kickbacks, misrepresentation in advertising, or pricefixing — *Factory Manager, Heavy Machinery.*

*   *

The paint industry is a highly competitive industry. Some pricecutting, but the ethics are generally high. The industry policy committee keeps watch on kickbacks. Safety is good in the larger corporations, but in the smaller ones it is not (there are few resources or expertise). Certain chemicals in paints are dangerous, but violations are minimal. There are many hazards in a paint plant, but "government looks over the shoulders," so there is little violation — *Assistant to Vice-President, Marketing Division, Paints*

The chemical industry is often misunderstood and thought by the public to be one or two of the worst — environmental violations, dumping of chemicals. The effects often were not known at the time. I doubt if most of it was intentional. The testing of effects of chemical products was well done. There was no pricefixing. There were kickbacks at the lower levels — *Plant Manager, Chemicals*

Good

I don't think any company could be "very good." In terms of the public interest, all corporations fail to make decisions in this manner. I often sat in on top management meetings and learned a lot. Pricefixing is a persistent problem in the heavy machinery industry. In sales to the utility market there was much unethical and perhaps even illegal corporate exchange of information so kickbacks, etc., were difficult; the industry was almost an open book — *General Manager, Heavy Machinery*

    *   *

Office machines is a very competitive business. Top management was generally quite ethical; sure as hell better than the auto industry. Like other businesses in the same areas there was pricefixing in the industry (on certain products). There were no kickbacks as a rule — *Executive Vice-President, International Production and Marketing, Office Machines*

    *   *

Industry has to watch its steps because of government in talking about prices, from whom you buy supplies, etc. There is an unwritten understanding between competitors that a person would not go with a competitor for 1-2 years, so industrial espionage was small. Some corporations in the industry are not quite so ethical. Some formulated products that were adulterated with worthless ingredients. Most of the major concerns tried to be honest in advertising, but there were some that were not — *Associate Director, Research and Development, Soaps*

    *   *

A fairly common practice has always been to give bribes (payola) to the disc jockeys to play company records. Not everyone is involved. Since regulations of government were established on this, compliance has been good — worker safety (e.g., working with dangerous chemical actions), some of them very toxic, has been good since the government got in on this too. Generally they have been fair to the artists. Patent suits between competitors are frequent. There was no pricefixing in the record industry — *Manager, Recording Development, Records*

*   *

Our industry (aerospace) was clean. The government was looking over our shoulders all the time. The industry is highly competitive. We must keep our noses clean or the corporations get into jeopardy. We must, however, play unethical "politics" in getting business (frequent "bribery" of government and military officials and political pressures are used) — *Contract Estimator, Aerospace*

Fair

Most of the aerospace industry is involved in government contracts. "Dog eat dog"; "lots of politics" in the industry, all competing to get contracts. There is entertainment of the military personnel. Retired military are later hired for contacts or as payoffs. The industry did things for officers attached to the plants, such as getting them free tickets, transportation, food and drink for football games, etc. Industry sponsored country club memberships, trips, etc., for the military to get contracts. They are all buttered up by the corporation. Some cost overruns are very unethical and even illegal, but one must recognize that they are often pioneer efforts and financial protection is needed for the corporation. The corporation tries to get in the door for a contract, then later costs grow and they knew that this would happen in advance. The work, however, is generally of the highest quality — *Manager, Systems Management, Aerospace*

*   *

Too much shoddy tire products, and the government later got in on this with tire standards. The public had been generally oversold on tires and did not get a break on guarantees and adjustments until the government got in. Pollution problems are great in factories. In the tire business generally there are no kickbacks — *Manager, Wholesale Department, Tires*

*   *

The oil industry is plagued with pricecutting. Some of it breaks the law. The oil industry is more inclined now to make a "fast buck" (it used to be on volume). Excessive pressures are put on dealers of large corporations (to keep open long hours, sales pressures, etc.) — *Regional Marketing Manager, Oil*

*   *

The corporations in the industry generally had a complete disregard for distributors and dealers. Distributors had quotas; corporations would often cancel the contract if they did not meet them. Generally the industry did not uphold good business ethics involving legitimate business practices. It generally would not hold pricing standard (had multiple prices), and not uphold service agreements (warranty). It endeavored generally, however, to build a good product, but some corporations did not — *Manager, Western Division Marketing, Appliances*

*   *

The industry lives on brand promotion. Claims and advertising are on borderline accuracy. Without the regulations of FTC the industry would have been a "dog eat dog" business — *Director, Business Development, Toiletries*

*   *

The auto industry tried formerly to give the public a good product at the best prices. It did not try to shove the product down your throat. More recently there has been price gouging. Ethics are not good today. Industrial espionage is very common in the auto industry, e.g., luring away a style engine or model maker — *General Purchasing Agent, Auto Industry*

EXECUTIVES' CORPORATIONS

Nearly three out of four respondents (73.0 percent) ranked their own corporations' ethics as "very good," and one out of five as "good." Only 6.3 percent ranked them as being "fair to poor." Corporate position made little difference in respondents' evaluations of their own corporations. For example, approximately three out of four executives in manufacturing and marketing ranked their corporations as "very good." Statistically, their responses were not significantly different in terms of either their treatment by a corporation or of the length of their retirement; in other words, a respondent who had been retired for a longer period of time was not more likely to have favorable memories of his corporation's ethics.

Considerable correspondence was found between the industry rankings and those given to the respondents' own corporations. For example, all who gave a "very good" rating to their own industries also gave the same to their own corporations. The correspondence on a "good" rating was 75.0 percent and 50.0 percent on a "fair" rating. All of the executives in the chemical and drug industries, as well as in the cosmetics industry, rated their corporations as very good, followed by the metal and motor vehicle industry. In general, the corporations given the lowest ratings were those in the industrial and farm equipment area.

Considering that the respondents' ranking of their own corporations' ethical standards was generally somewhat higher than that of the industrywide standards, the question can be raised as to the underlying reasons for this diversity. Was it due to feelings of corporate loyalty, did they not have a complete picture of other corporations' ethics, or were their corporations actually operating on a higher ethical standard?

An attempt was made to compare the respondents' ratings of their own corporations with the data provided in a previous study of Fortune 500 illegalities (Clinard et al., 1979). This study had covered the two-year period, 1975-1976, when most of the corporate executives were still actively employed. The corporations in the sample were checked to see how they had appeared in this ranking, and a comparative rating scale was devised that involved government actions initiated during this period for all violations and for serious-to-moderate violations (for definitions, see Clinard et al., 1979: 76-77). The serious-to-moderate violations were given a double weight in the combined scale. Those Fortune 500 corporations considered to be "very good" stood less than 300th in the violation scale, those with a ranking between 101 and 300 were considered "good," and those in the top 100 corporations were considered to be "fair-to-poor." If anything, therefore, corporations in the "fair-to-poor" category were given a broader distribution than if they were confined to the top 50 of the 500.

According to this rating scale, of the 64 cases studied (51 actual corporations), nearly two out of three (60.9 percent) were rated "very good" or "good," with one out of three (32.8 percent) rated "very good." Slightly more than one-fourth (26.6 percent) were ranked as "fair-to-poor." Statistical comparison showed considerable similarity between the two corporation ratings, although there was a tendency for the scale ratings of the corporations to be slightly lower than those of the executives.[2] Two-thirds (62.5 percent) of the corporations rated "very good" by the executives were rated "good" on the scale. One-fifth (21.8 percent) of the corporations rated "good" were also rated "good" on the scale, while exactly one-half of those corporations rated as "fair-to-poor" were found to be "fair-to-poor" on the scale. Again, the actual comparison was of the executives' ratings of the ethics of a given corporation with our scale, based on violations. "Ethics" was defined to include violations. There would have been little difference had we compared the ratings on corporate violations, inasmuch as they were almost the same as for ethics; if anything, they were slightly better.

The executives gave a variety of reasons for their favorable comments about their corporations. They were, in order of ranking: (1) their corporation was highly ethical and had few violations; (2) the ethical standard was higher than that of their competitors or of the industry as a whole; (3) the corporation was fair to customers; (4) the product safety record was good; (5) worker safety was emphasized; and (6) the procedures of internal auditing largely prevented violations. The respondents who mentioned various negative aspects of their own corporations pointed particularly to monopolistic practices, pricefixing, illegal bribery and political contributions, lack of attention to worker safety, EEOC (Equal Employment Opportunity Commission) violations, and the prevalence of kickbacks.

Additional comments brought out the following points about many corporations that were considered to be highly ethical: (1) if the founder of the corporation was highly ethical, a general ethical pattern was set for the corporation to follow; (2) if the top managers had risen from the ranks, rather than being brought in from outside, a high level of corporate standards was more likely to be set; (3) ethical patterns were better in cases where the government had at one time taken strong action against the corporation; (4) ethical standards were better if top management made a strong effort with internal audits, specific communication from top management, and frequent meetings with middle management; and (5) the likelihood of dismissal for unethical or illegal practices within the corporation led to higher ethical standards. The following excerpts illustrate these points. (It must be noted that many of the corporations which respondents had ranked as "very good" or "good" did engage in some unethical practices.)

Very Good

There were rigorous procedures to see that we complied with government regulations. For example, after the passage of the Foreign Corrupt Practices Act a regular "Gestapo" was set up — whenever you opened a drawer a lawyer popped out. We had a written code of ethics, and there was much in-house auditing of operations to see that we were conforming to this code — *Manager, International Operations, Chemicals*

*   *

It was a good, honest corporation. The founder was a very ethical man, and later top management followed his views. The corporation grew slowly and this helped to maintain the original high ethical standards. We did, however, have to give a "voluntary" percent of our salary to political contributions — *Plant Manager, Automotive Parts*

*   *

Our corporation was very strict on ethics. The awareness of ethical standards by top management came down from the founder — *Manager, Business Practices, Business Equipment*

*   *

The ethics were very good compared with the rest of the industry; the corporation made an effort to be ethical. We put more money into product research than did other corporations. Our brand names were very important, and we wanted to protect them and have consumers willing to buy our products — *Director, Business Development, Toiletries*

*   *

Sometimes our corporation went too far to be ethical. They leaned over backwards to conform to government regulations. Following World War I, though, the corporation was involved in some criticism for excessive profits. Trust busting (under Theodore Roosevelt) broke us into three companies back in about 1910. We had been criticized as a monopoly and later we had to be careful in our ethics — *District Sales Manager, Chemicals*

*   *

My corporation would not give kickbacks, even in foreign countries. The corporation tried to keep clear of FDA and FTC in advertising; we always had technical evidence to support our claims — *Associate Director, Research and Development, Soaps*

*   *

Our ethics were about the same as in the industry. We were involved in some bribery in foreign countries. In testing pharmaceuticals I was always sure, as I did not want to go to jail. In drug shipments ("contributions") to Cuba after the Bay of Pigs, as a ransom that totaled $50 million by the industry, we were allowed a tax deduction which actually the public paid for. We took out-of-date drugs, etc., and shipped them, but we got the people home. Are corporations cheating in a case like this? — *Director, Corporate Services, Pharmaceuticals*

*   *

We made a quality product. The parent corporation had been long ago under a consent decree and after that we were told to "watch things" in our acquired company — *Vice President, Manufacturing Division, Paper*

*   *

Top management people had high standards, and this filtered down. I'm not too familiar with the corporation marketing practices. We had lots of staff meetings at all levels and with top management. Memoranda from top management often would come down to comply with the regulations and the spirit of the regulations. Some regulations, however, are subject to corporate interpretation as on oil pricing, etc., and we might have been in violation — *Supervisor, Employee Benefit Plans, Oil*

*   *

We cooperated with the government in compliance with regulations such as OSHA. Our executives also helped government agencies with their problems. Training was given to middle management on ethics and an ethical philosophy trickled down from top management. We had frequent advice and counseling from legal counsel. I know nothing unethical done in my corporation. If there were bad judgments we did not try to cover up. Our corporation had a cease and desist order on pricefixing (with Sears) in 1935, and the effects of this carried on over the years. This indicates often the importance over time of an important cease and desist order — *Operations Manager, Tires*

*   *

The corporation was fair to customers and the public. Excellent compliance with government regulations. Part of our good ethical standards was the Quaker origin of the founders; top management subsequently followed this tradition (one in top management said that in any deal it must be fair to both the customer and to the competitor). Part of our good ethics was self-preservation because of the dangerous chemicals that we produced — there was the possibility of consumer suits and government action. Three-fourths of top management came up from the ranks. Most were long-term employees so that ethical standards had to be maintained — *Director, Corporate Taxes, Chemicals*

*   *

One of the highest in ethical standards in the entire steel industry. Not engaged in foreign payoffs. Had specific policy statement on corporate ethics and also social responsibility. Founder's ethical tradition carried on in the corporation (founder's father was a minister) with family carry-over in top management and on the Board of Directors. Corporation carried on business through "using Christian principles." Corporation was so concerned with safety in the plant that it even has sent out safety suggestions to retirees — *Manager, International Division, Steel*

*   *

Every corporation takes on the character of the person who founded it — in our case he was a small-town boy and very ethical. The whole corporation afterward tended to be ethical as it split into divisions and grew with this trend. Divisions were small enough to discover unethical practices of middle management — *National Accounts Manager, Health Supplies*

*   *

The people at top management were not dishonest in anything. All were good people. It was assumed that we would comply with government regulations. Government contracts were treated the same as commercial contracts (the government was not ripped off). No worker safety problems — *Cost Accountant, Special Products Division, Electrical*

*   *

One time we had a chance to sell 15,000 tons a month on a kickback, but they knew the standards of the company on ethics. I told them, "So don't talk to me about it" — *Marketing Manager, European Division, Food*

*   *

Outstanding in ethics. If we were caught doing anything unethical we had no opportunity to resign but were fired. There were letters each year from the corporation president with guidelines, and ethics was one of them. People were not allowed to accept *any* gifts at all levels. Communication down the line in the corporation was good. Videotapes from corporation on various corporate issues were sent to plants to show to employees. It was originally a family corporation with top management usually a tightly held group. Top management generally came up from the ranks, and the corporation seldom went outside even for members of the Board of Directors. When they were from outside they generally had specialized knowledge of value to the corporation — *Plant Manager, Chemicals*

*   *

One president of our corporation said you have several obligations: (1) God, (2) country, (3) family, (4) corporation. Any trouble would endanger the reputation of the corporation. I was told: "Remember, you are working for a first-rate company. You are expected to live like that and act like that" — *Manager, Employee Benefits, Aluminum*

Good

The son of the founder was chairman when I started, and our policies took into consideration the stockholders, the employees, and the public. The corporate situation has deteriorated since that time. This is also true of business ethics in general — *Director, Business Development, Farm Equipment*

*   *

Our corporation's founder was succeeded by his son; both had high ethical standards, and corporation's top management continued to follow their standards. We built a better product. We bent over backward to make adjustments without government interference. One reason was our highly developed research and development rather than top management's efforts. At one time top management bled the corporation for the stockholders. No kickbacks or illegal rebates given by our corporation — *General Counsel, Tires*

*   *

We were charged in 1954 with not allowing competitor purchases (Robinson-Patman Act). A consent decree forced the corporation to divest as constituting a monopoly. The decree forced us to shape up. Twice a year our officials met with U.S. Department of Justice officials to see if they were in violation — *General Counsel, Food*

Fair

The ethics of my own corporation, like the industry in general, was "dog eat dog." Problems grew out of government regulations to control certain accepted unethical industry practices and also excessive competition. Payoffs, kickbacks, etc., were all part of the business — *Director, Public Relations, Food*

*   *

The big thing was cost overruns on government contracts. Costs were often switched or charged to other projects. For example, the cost of research and development was spread over all projects even though a particular project was not involved. We promised to meet schedules that we never intended to keep. My division was always dependent on government and the securing of contracts was important. We were more ethical than some in the aerospace industry. We were careful about entertaining the military — we even made them pay for their own luncheons — *Budget Coordinators, Aerospace*

*   *

Our ethics were not the best and not the worst in the industry. I was told always to "hammer down" the price of purchases so the corporation might make sufficient profits (the corporation, for example, would not even pay the freight costs). This was typical;

our corporation practiced tight margins, and this affected ethical practices. The corporation changed top management continually. Dealers had to make sales quotas; corporation pressures were great so the dealer had to "almost give it away." When OSHA inspectors (e.g., electrical) would find something wrong, the supervisors would tend to say, "Just ignore them" — *General Purchasing Agent, Auto Industry*

VIOLATIONS OF GOVERNMENT REGULATIONS

Shifting from the more general question regarding the respondents' views of their own corporations' ethics, a more specific question was asked about the degree of their corporations' violations of the law and of government regulations. Three out of four (77.8 percent) said that these were not extensive, while 17.5 percent replied that they were fairly extensive, and 4.7 percent believed that they were extensive. No significant difference was found between their responses and how they felt they were treated by the corporation. For example, one-third (33.3 percent) of those who felt that the violations were extensive thought that they had been treated well by the corporation, compared with only 26.5 percent of those who felt that the violations were not extensive. Length of retirement was not statistically significant.

In view of the frequent negative views about marketing expressed by those in manufacturing, it was surprising that nearly all of the executives in marketing felt that the violations in their corporations were not extensive, as compared with about two-thirds (61.9 percent) of those in manufacturing. The executives who felt most strongly that violations were not extensive in their corporations were from metals, electronics and appliances, and chemical industries. Generally, executives in the oil industry believed that violations were extensive in their corporations.

Respondents who believed that there were no extensive violations attributed this situation largely to the role of top management, to corporation "self-policing" through the efforts of their legal counsels and frequent meetings between top and middle management, and to the physical location of their corporations. Others pointed out the salutory effect, over the years, of a strong previous government action. Some of the corporations had persons at the top management level assigned specifically to problems of safety, financial problems, and the like, while others assigned a person to visit Washington in order to discuss regulations, both old and new, and to learn how best to comply with them. Because of the fear of losing future contracts, corporations holding government contracts tried to comply strictly with regulations of the EPA, OSHA, and so forth. Nevertheless, the practice of defrauding the government on their contracts, through cost overruns, was reported to be fairly common. Some of the respondents' replies were:

> We rarely tangled with the law. There were complaints about the law, but not violations. Top management accounted for this. For a hundred years my corporation was a family affair, and an effort was made to preserve the family reputation — *Associate Director, Research and Development, Soaps*

> *   *

> There were few violations because each year all middle management, including plant managers, tried to hold a conference with top management where we could talk both ways. New laws were discussed by someone from the general counsel's office who would come to the plant. There were written guidelines on the regulations and how they affected the company, and corporate guidelines were set up — *Plant Manager, Automotive Parts*

> *   *

> Violations were not extensive because my corporation policed things themselves (it had policies) through internal audit and through people coming out constantly from the home office — *Director, Business Development, Farm Equipment*

> *   *

> There were ethical problems, but not in violations of government regulations. We had a legal department (very costly to the corporation) that kept us out of trouble. Labor unions also policed us; they had very strong attitudes, particularly in regard to worker safety — *Manager, Manufacturing Facility Planning*

> *   *

> The corporation had a strict regard for all rules and regulations (except Nixon political campaign contributions). There was

enough discipline in every division. Corporation kept track of receipts and persons could hardly give kickbacks. A general manager's conference was held quarterly with top management to discuss government regulations and other corporate problems — *National Accounts Manager, Health Care*

*   *

Our corporation accepted regulations in general. We had representatives who went to Washington to find out the purposes of the regulations, etc., the goals, and also to become educated so as to comply with the regulations. We tried to find out where we failed in our own efforts that would make a government regulation necessary (e.g., what was wrong with our claims based on our research on new products) — *Labor Relations and Personnel Administration, Chemicals*

*   *

After a big pricefixing case and the corporation was convicted, there were no more such cases. After that we generally complied with government regulations. We had an "employee-oriented corporation," and this helped to keep down violations. The type of local community had a lot to do with compliance (both Milwaukee and West Allis are conservative, well-run cities, and this has had a lot to do with compliance). Since we were a multi-plant company, one could test this — some other communities where our plants were located had more violations; the cities had different characteristics and were more often also "problem communities" — *General Manager, Heavy Machinery*

*   *

It was difficult to have violations since nearly all were government contracts. If we violated various government regulations it might mean that we would not get another government contract. There could be, however, "cross-charges" on several contracts (e.g., charging costs of one project to another). We would have cross-audits to catch these violations by the supervisory or the purchasing staffs. One could cheat on quality and falsifying of records. We would rather face an overrun, however, than to cheat on quality. OSHA, EEOC violations were rare because of government contracts — *Manager, Systems Management, Aerospace*

Respondents who thought that violations were either fairly extensive or extensive stated that their corporations followed the rather general industrywide patterns of violations, that monopolistic practices, safety, and OSHA violations were more frequent, and that many violations occurred because there were just too many government regulations with which they were expected to comply. Their comments dealt less with preventive actions and more with the role of the government's enforcement of regulations. Some typical comments are the following:

> There was much collusion on pricefixing. Talking with other companies, either competitors or dealers, about allocation of supplies was common. It is hard to have price conversations with competitors without law violations — *Regional Marketing Manager, Oil*

> *   *

> In case an OSHA inspector, for example in electrical work, would find something wrong, the supervisors would tend to say just to ignore them. Our corporation disregarded certain government regulations up to a point. OSHA worker safety was the most likely violation — *General Purchasing Agent, Auto Industry*

> *   *

> OSHA found many safety violations in our plants, and EPA violations resulted in numerous recalls. Also NHTSA standards were broken — *Advanced Design Engineer, Auto Industry*

In summary, the middle management executives tended to give favorable ratings to the ethical standards of both their own industries and their own corporations. They also maintained that on the whole, compliance with the law and with government regulations was good. Moreover, the ethical ratings given their own corporations were in general agreement with actual data on violations from another study. On the other hand, the favorable ratings given their own corporations often conflicted with specific comments about unethical behavior and corporate law violations. Of particular interest were their opinions about why their own corporations were ethical or not, an issue to be examined more fully in the next chapter.

NOTES

1. All analyses of comments are presented in order of frequency or magnitude. All executive comments were typed on individual cards, then coded. Computer

analyses were made of the total responses and, in some cases, the first responses made to the question.

2. Tests of statistical significance using chi squares were not possible here, as in many other cases, because of the size of the sample. The distribution showed too many cells with fewer than five cases. Consequently, in all further analyses no mention will be made of tests of statistical significance unless they were valid.

4

$W_{HY}\ S_{OME}\ C_{ORPORATIONS}\ A_{RE}$
$M_{ORE}\ E_{THICAL\ THAN}\ O_{THERS}$

The middle management executives interviewed here had been a part of the corporate world for an average of a third of a century. In view of their lengthy corporate experience, they were asked: "Why do you think that some large corporations are unethical and violate the law a great deal, while others appear to be ethical and seldom violate the law?" They were asked not only about their own corporations and industries, but about the corporate world as a whole. Their responses were analyzed in two ways — by the first or immediate answer given by each executive, and then by their total responses, since most of them gave more than one reason.

TOP MANAGEMENT

As their first answer, most of the executives said that top management was the chief explanation for corporate violations (53.1 percent), either due to unethical behavior or personal ambition. (see Table 4.1). Second was competition and greed, and third, the type of industry.

When all 125 responses (an average of nearly two per executive) are considered, top management accounted for approximately the same proportion (51.2 percent), but to this was added the factor of poor supervision (see Table 4.2). Second was competition, and third, type of industry, the same as for the first response.

TABLE 4.1   First Response to Why Some Corporations Are More Ethical than Others

Reason	N	Percentage
Top management	34	53.1
Ethics	(31)	(48.4)
Personal ambition	(3)	(4.7)
Competition, greed	13	20.3
Type of industry	7	10.9
Ethical history of corporation	4	6.3
Financial problems	2	3.1
Unfamiliarity with the law	2	3.1
Disregard of customer	1	1.6
Other	1	1.6
Total	64	100.0

Using only first responses, almost half (48.4 percent) of the respondents said that the differences between corporations were due largely to the ethics of top management, particularly the CEO (Chief Executive Officer). Many felt that top management's ethics declined (1) when there was no orderly transition in top management, as for example, when personnel failed to be upgraded from within the corporate ranks; (2) when a CEO or president was hired from outside the corporation, and (3) when top management personnel were more interested in the money and prestige of their position than in the reputation of the corporation. A sharp distinction was drawn between CEOs who were "financially oriented" and those "professionally oriented."

> As a mirror reflects an object, so top management reflects the corporation. If top management sees to it that government regulations are complied with, middle management will do it. The board of directors is sometimes not strong, so it has little influence on the ethics of a corporation — *General Manager, Marketing, Steel*

*   *

> The final decision on ethics is made by top management of the corporation. Maybe only one or two in the top management are

TABLE 4.2   Total Responses to Why Some Corporations Are More Ethical than Others

Reasons	N	Percentage
Top management	64	51.2
Ethics	(52)	(41.6)
Personal ambition	(9)	(7.2)
Poor supervision	(3)	(2.4)
Competition, greed, profits	18	14.4
Type of industry	14	11.2
Ethical history of corporation	8	6.4
Financial difficulties	6	4.8
Employees' familiarity with the law	5	4.0
Disregard of customers	2	1.6
Other	8	6.4
Total	125	100.0

involved, but they can set the standards for middle management — *Executive Vice President, Foods*

*   *

Top management is responsible for whether a corporation is unethical or ethical. Top management wants to be surrounded by persons who follow their ideas and patterns of behavior — *Sales Manager, Parts Division, Business Machines*

*   *

Top management is the main reason for ethical and unethical corporate practices. If we had a change in the CEO, etc., we could sense the difference all the way down the ranks. Most CEOs, unfortunately, came from sales and made ethical decisions in terms of sales. Middle management reacted to ethical principles from above — *Manager, Manufacturing Facility Planning, Farm Equipment*

*   *

An orderly procedure of top management change enables handing down procedures that are well defined and the philosophy of the way to do business. Some corporations bring in those with drastically opposite views (e.g., some companies can be wrecked by a change in management). A tower of strength in top management can be replaced by a weak one, or the corporation will go outside the corporation for someone because top management has not brought up competent men — *Associate Director, Research and Development, Soaps*

*   *

The direction and morality of top management is generally involved in ethics and violations. The CEO who says that there are not ethical or violation problems in his corporation that he knows about is a bad supervisor — *Executive Vice President, International Production and Marketing, Office Machines*

*   *

Top management are the ones who set the pace within the corporation. If they permit violations either they do not exercise proper control or exercise proper leadership — *Manager, International Division, Steel*

*   *

The difference in corporate ethics is entirely dependent on the nature of persons in top management or sometimes in middle management. The extent of pride in the corporation has a lot to do with it; also how they select and train middle management for top management — *Manager, International Government Relations, Oil*

The importance of top management's personal ambition was mentioned by 4.7 percent of the respondents. This also included their efforts to keep their present positions and their executive perks (perquisites).

Some top management executives try to look "super," have high egos, and want power and success. They tell middle management to do certain unethical behavior or violations and keep their mouths shut — *Systems Engineer Coordinator with Marketing, Electronics*

*   *

The personality of the CEO or the president is important, particularly if he is a rugged individualist or a "Go-Go" type. He thinks the corporation must be first, with no holds barred. Such persons build conglomerates. There is an overriding desire to be a corporation that is "number one" in profits and in securing profits for the stockholders — *Contract Estimator, Aerospace*

   *   *

Our CEO was a technical man, an engineer, and not a financially oriented man interested in the fast buck — *Manager, Management Engineering, Aerospace*

   *   *

Violations are likely if top management is seeking to advance their personal reputations and be "hot shots." Those in top management in corporations who stay out of trouble assume the social responsibility for their products' safety and depend upon the general counsel to advise them on how to keep out of trouble — *Director, Business Development, Toiletries*

   *   *

Corporations with many violations are being run primarily for the top and bottom line in order to make a buck. The personalities of top management, particularly the CEO, is important; if a person is crooked at the top this can affect middle management — *Plant Manager, Chemicals*

   *   *

The corporation's desire to be No. 1 makes for violations; there are some money-hungry corporations — *Manager, Operations, Food*

   *   *

Some top management think that they are smarter than the government and think that they can get away with it. Someone will risk his personal reputation to attract a favorable reaction from the Board of Directors by showing a good profit record — *Manager, Operations, Foods*

   *   *

Some top management are ethical and some are not. How they get there does not mean that they were ethical in doing so — some climb over the backs of others with "steel plates in their shoes" — *Plant Manager, Automotive Parts*

   *   *

Greed and a grab for power by top management accounts for many violations. In my corporation it was the Vice President for Marketing who encouraged violations of the law — *Director, Public Relations, Foods*

*   *

My personal feeling is that those corporations that are unethical are managed by persons (CEOs) who are highly competitive, wanting to improve the corporation's profit margins and thinking that they will not get caught. Such CEOs are trying to improve their personal positions and that of their corporation. The only way to do it is often unethical — *Labor Relations and Personnel Administration, Chemicals*

*   *

Upper management structure, particularly the CEO, leads to unethical practices. They are the "Go-Go" type of managers. Such a CEO does not intend to stay for more than two years, and he cares little about the corporation's reputation. Like sharks they gobble up other corporations. Such CEOs end up with lots of executive perks and their names are favorably mentioned as go-getters in *The Wall Street Journal* and in *Fortune* — *Manager, Management Engineering, Aerospace*

*   *

Those corporations which have had troubles with illegal behavior have had a CEO who was a "scamp" or one or two others in top management. They want a killing for themselves, they raid the corporation, and they make fast deals — *Director, Corporate Taxes, Chemicals*

COMPETITION AND GREED

The second largest response (20.3 percent) was that the difference is due to the degree of competition and greed of certain corporations, some of whom are aggressive in trying to show profits and thus put greater pressures on sales people.

All corporations are primarily interested in making a profit. Some are more "aggressive" than others and violate the law. After all, this is a capitalist system. This is difficult to answer generally, however, as each industry group varies — *Manager, Marketing Support, Aerospace*

*   *

All corporations are profit-making companies; if things do not go right they do not stay in the business. Very competitive areas are those in which there are more likely to be violations — *Manager, Operations, Supply and Distribution, Auto Industry*

*   *

More aggressive corporations take chances and violate the law, while more conservative corporations tend not to take chances. They might like to do so but because of their reputations and their not wanting to get involved with the law they do not — *Manager, Recording Division, Records*

TYPES OF INDUSTRY

The third largest response (10.9 percent) was that the type of industry was of great importance, as some industries are more ethical than are others, and industry standards are reflected in the ethical behavior of many corporations.

In violations the type of industry is important in terms of the kinds of products they sell and how much profit is in it for them. If there is a low profit margin there may be more corporate violations — *Manager, Wholesale Department, Tires*

*   *

Some industries like oil are more given to violations — *Manager, Public Relations, Building Materials*

*   *

Violations are characteristic of some industries that are highly competitive, such as the paper industry. It becomes a way of doing business in the industry. It is tolerated by top management — *Division Manager, Light Machinery*

ETHICAL HISTORY OF THE CORPORATION

The fourth reason given (6.3 percent) was the importance of the ethical history of the corporation, with particular emphasis on the role of its founder.

> The history of the company and its founder (in my company it was the founder's family, and it was ethically oriented). Later they attracted this kind of people in top management — *Director, Research Administration, Chemicals*

*   *

> Many violations are a reflection of those in top management. If the founder of the corporation or president or CEO were unethical, middle management will be also. Also a decline in profits or other financial pinches such as cash flow might lead to unethical practices or to violations of law — *Factory Manager, Heavy Machinery*

*   *

> The son of the corporation's founder as CEO was highly ethical as well as others in top management. They had high corporate ethical standards. The conduct of middle management is the result of the ability of top management to pick other ethical persons — *Manager, Agricultural Relations, Tires*

*   *

> It goes back to the beginning of the corporation. If the founder had high ethical standards it sets a corporation pattern of doing business. This is particularly true of corporations where the family connections carry over into top management — *Marketing Manager, European Division, Foods*

FINANCIAL DIFFICULTIES

It was particularly significant that the executives interviewed ranked in fifth place the fact that a corporation's financial situation, such as a decline in corporate profits, might lead to violations. Among the comments pointing to the importance of financial problems were:

> Top management's attempt to get its investment money back as quickly as possible might force them to do some unethical and

illegal things to meet competition in some cases — *Senior Process Engineer, Electrical*

*   *

Most of the time difference is "the bottom line" in order to get profits where pressures are great — either the corporation is losing money, not getting as much as they want, or they are not getting their proper share of the market — *Materials Manager, Light Machinery*

*   *

Much illegal behavior in a corporation is an act of financial desperation when losing money or position in the industry — *Manager, Advanced Engineering Facilities, Auto Industry*

Various other explanations were given: The employees of some corporations are better trained in law and regulations, and some corporations care less than others about the consumer. An unusual reason was given by one interviewee who said that corporations whose home offices are located in smaller communities tend to be more ethical than those located in large cities. In a small community, the possibility is greater that others will know more about what is going on and, with the corporation's reputation at stake, fewer chances will be taken to risk violations of the law. Much the same conclusion was reached by Lane (1953/1977) when he sought to explain the various law violations in the New England shoe industry.

UNFAIR COMPETITIVE PRACTICES

Unethical corporate behavior, including violations of the law, is commonly believed to be greatly affected by the unfair competitive pressures of corporations that do engage in unethical practices. Corporate management may see their competitors making greater profits through various unethical means, possibly even breaking the law and getting away with it. As a result, a previously ethical corporation might lower the quality of its products, violate certain regulations of agencies like the EEOC, EPA, OSHA, and others. In the marketing area, they might give illegal kickbacks and rebates, or they might make foreign payoffs in order to obtain contracts more easily.

Although the pressures of competition, in answer to an open-ended question, ranked second on the list of causative factors that may explain unethical corporate practices and violations, a different view was found when the question was directed specifically at unfair competitive practices. Most middle management (58.7 percent) then responded that the unethical competitive practices of other corporations had little or no effect on the behavior of ethical corporations. Of those who took this view, 39.7 percent said that there was little effect, and 19.0 percent thought there was no effect. Nearly one-third (29.7 percent) felt that competitive practices did have some effect. A much larger proportion of those in manufacturing corporations (52.4 percent) felt that competitive practices play a role in unethical practices than in marketing corporations (33.4 percent), which is not the situation that one might expect considering the frequent charges of unfair marketing practices. Executives from the aerospace and chemical industries were the most likely to believe that unfair competition was a factor in violations; least likely to believe this to be so were executives from the drug and cosmetics industries.

In all, one-fourth (25.7 percent of the total comments) of the respondents stated that unethical corporations do not influence the practices of ethical ones. In fact, some went so far as to claim that large ethical corporations could force out unscrupulous competitors if they wished to do so. Others went even further, insisting that some corporations that raised the issue of unfair competition by others were only doing so to cover up their own violations. Still others felt that the behavior of unethical corporations, once revealed to consumers, might increase the business of the ethical ones. Finally, it was pointed out that the presence of government regulations keeps the ethical corporations conscious of their reputations and "in line" in spite of unfair competitor pressures.

I think that the practices of competitors are not a significant factor in the unethical or illegal behavior of a corporation — *Manager, Recording Development, Records*

*   *

An ethical corporation does not respond to the unethical behavior of other corporations — *Director, Business Development, Farm Equipment*

*   *

Even if business is lost this would not drive an ethical corporation into unethical practices — *District Sales Manager, Steel*

*   *

A corporation that has a very good product can hold the market without being unethical. This includes the quality that goes into the product — *Manager, Automotive Marketing Division, Auto Industry*

*   *

Unethical competition really does a favor to an ethical corporation in that it brings in more business to others (e.g., Firestone's unethical practices in the tire industry) — *Operations Manager, Tires*

*   *

Government regulations and penalties help to hold the ethical corporation in check so they do not follow the behavior of unethical corporations — *General Counsel, Foods*

*   *

Corporations that are dishonest and want to show an increase in profits tend to be unethical or violate the law. Their practices would not affect an ethical and profitable corporation — *Manager, Western Division Marketing, Appliances*

*   *

If it is a very large corporation, the ethics of small competing firms have little influence — *Systems Engineer, Coordinator with Marketing, Electronics*

*   *

The unethical practices of other corporations are a poor excuse for unethical practices — *Marketing Manager, European Division, Foods*

Only one out of nine respondents felt that unfair or illegal competitive practices contribute much or very much to unethical behavior in that corporations must engage in them in order to remain competitive. Those who felt that they have some effect believed that unfair competition was a factor, but that the only influence was from major competitors. Other respondents felt that such practices have an effect only in certain industries, such as the aerospace industry.

It is hard to keep salesmen under control when others are doing such things as giving kickbacks, etc. — *District Sales Manager, Chemicals*

*   *

It forces corporations in many cases to be unethical or to violate the law, as in the auto industry — *Assistant to Vice President, Manufacturing, Paints*

*   *

Corporations have to be cost-competitive — *Supervisor, Employee Benefit Plans, Oil*

*   *

Competition plays a role in unethical behavior and in violations, but it does not happen as much as the anti-business community thinks it does — *General Manager, Heavy Machinery*

*   *

It forces ethical corporations to meet, to some extent, their unethical competition. Some corporations, however, can resist this type of competition — *Manager, Management Engineering, Aerospace*

*   *

Some top ethical corporations will sometimes follow the practices of others who are unethical — *Manager, Operations, Foods*

*   *

An ethical corporation cannot compete at a disadvantage; if some are gaining profits from their practices it is hard for other corporations to avoid it themselves — *Manager, Business Practices, Business Equipment*

*   *

If, in our corporation, we found that at General Motors they were doing something in violation of the law and getting away with it, we adopted it. Similar situations also occurred among smaller firms supplying our corporation — *General Purchasing Agent, Auto Industry*

*   *

As in the extensive pricefixing in the corrugated box industry, some corporations can be influenced by the behavior of others — *Executive Vice President, Foods*

*   *

To some extent unethical practices do affect other corporations, for example, foreign payoffs by one corporation may force the others to do likewise — *Manager, International Marketing Division, Chemicals*

*   *

Unethical practices by others could affect an ethical corporation. But the reverse situation can also happen where an ethical corporation can drive out an unethical one with the quality of their products and public relations statements about their ethical practices and work conditions — *Plant Manager, Chemicals*

CORPORATION CULTURE — ETHICAL AND UNETHICAL

As pointed out (see p. 23), some believe that the culture of a corporation tends to be ethical or unethical in its nature, a characteristic that is often even more important than the influence of top management. This view was supported to a degree, but it was not firmly established. About two-thirds of the executives (59.4 percent) felt that some corporations do have a generally ethical or unethical culture, but 40.6 percent disagreed. A somewhat larger percentage (68.0 percent) in marketing felt that the corporate culture was of more significance than did those in the manufacturing area (57.1 percent). The respondents who felt most strongly about the importance of a corporate culture were from the chemical industry.

The majority of those who felt that corporations do have an ethical history pointed out that the basic principles of a corporation's founder, or some subsequent powerful top management figure, can have a marked long-term influence, and that once a corporate pattern of ethics is established, it is difficult to change, regardless of top management. Again, several pointed out that the location of corporate headquarters in a smaller city helps greatly to maintain ethical traditions, since big cities in themselves tend to have an unethical milieu. The following comments are typical of the executives who felt that corporate culture can have long-term effects:

> Some corporations have an ethical or unethical history, and they bring in from the outside a type of top management that will fit into the corporation's pattern. Top management could change, and this might change the corporate pattern, but this does not happen much. In an unethical corporation a new ethical CEO wants to "sweep with a broom," but everyone else sweeps things under the rug away from him so that he cannot change things. Once practices have been established in a corporation, it is difficult to change them — *General Manager, Heavy Machinery*

>   *   *

> Some corporations are more ethical because of a corporation history and possibly their location in a smaller community rather than in a larger one — *Director, Research Administration, Chemical*

>   *   *

> A corporation's history often starts from the original founders and their ethical standards, from the beginning, prevail; for example, corporate reputation means a lot to some, similar to that of a Japanese corporation — *Operations Manager, Tires*

>   *   *

> Some corporations once had top management, often the founder, that was either ethical or unethical. This established a continuity at the beginning. It can start out well, or the reverse may be the case. If a corporation has long practiced unethical or ethical behavior, a CEO may find it difficult to change — *Production Director, Tires*

>   *   *

> There are still some corporations that are ethical over long periods of time, regardless of top management's influence. This

will change as today's young corporate executives want to get ahead rapidly, and will crawl over the backs of anyone to get ahead — *Manager, Systems Management, Aerospace*

*   *

With respect to a general ethical culture, it is true for the ones that are ethical, but I am not as sure that there are culturally unethical corporations — *Manager, International Division, Steel*

*   *

Some corporations want to protect their reputations more than others do — *Manager, Advanced Engineering Facilities, Records*

*   *

Often corporations develop a way of doing business unethically, and it takes a lot at the top to change it — *Manager, Advanced Engineering Facilities, Automotive Parts*

*   *

Top management, particularly the CEO, could change an ethical corporation, but it would have a hard time. People below (middle management) would already be indoctrinated — *Marketing Manager, European Division, Foods*

*   *

Those corporations that are new and do not have a tradition or reputation to uphold tend to get into trouble — *Manager, International Marketing Division, Chemicals*

*   *

I think there are some corporations with an ethical standard that is passed on to employees as they become top management, and then they in turn pass them on, and so on. On the other hand, some corporations say "a little shady business is OK" — *Division Sales Manager, Oil*

In the opinion of the executives who denied the existence of corporate cultures, the general tone of being ethical or unethical was not thought to be due to corporate history but rather to the general characteristics of top management. The following comments typify their responses:

> Ethics comes and goes in a corporation according to who is in top management. I worked under four corporation presidents, and each differed — first was honest, next was a "wheeler-dealer," the third was somewhat better, and the last one was bad. According to their ethical views, pressures were put on middle management all the way down — *General Counsel, Foods*

>   *   *

> My experiences are that it is chiefly top management, particularly the CEO, rather than a cultural tradition of the corporation. Corporations, as such, are generally not ethical or unethical — *Manager, Manufacturing Facility Planning, Farm Equipment*

>   *   *

> There are no unethical corporations, but only unethical top management — *Cost Accountant, Special Products Division, Electric*

In a sense, the question of corporate culture versus top management is not a clear-cut distinction, inasmuch as a corporation with a long-term ethical tradition may tend to select CEOs, for example, who fit well into the corporate pattern, whereas the reverse may well be true of corporations characterized by an unethical culture. Top management reflects the way a corporation wants to do business. When one includes this position, the importance of a clear-cut corporate culture diminishes and the role of top management increases. Others introduced a different dimension, namely that an ethical or unethical culture is sometimes rooted in industry methods of doing business rather than in specific corporations.

> Really, it is the interaction between the corporation and ultimately top management; the interaction between the two is deeper than top management. "Birds of a feather flock together." That is, corporations with unethical principles attract such top management. The Board of Directors can be active or not in such situations — *Manager, Employee Benefits, Aluminum*

>   *   *

Some corporations have a history and attract top management and middle management to fit their corporation's culture of unethical or ethical practices — *Manager, Wholesale Department, Tires*

*   *

Not only corporations but industries can be characterized by ethical and unethical practices. Corporations in certain industries tend to select top management who fit the way the corporation wants business to be conducted — *Plant Manager, Chemicals*

*   *

In some types of industries top management thinks the practices are necessary, for example, in the aircraft and oil industries. Violations are tied up with the production and the sale of certain commodities in certain industries — *Executive Vice President, International Production and Marketing, Office Machines*

*   *

Some corporations in certain industries as such have a bad record, for example, the large oil corporations. Generally it is an industry, but it can be individual corporations — *Assistant to Vice President, Manufacturing, Paints*

*   *

Certain industries and corporations are more prone to get into trouble — they have a history of doing so — *Division Manager, Machinery*

*   *

Most corporations are largely unethical, but it varies by industry — *Plant Manager, Aluminum*

In summary, most of the executives believed that unethical corporate behavior can usually be traced to internal rather than external forces. Internally, individual ethics, personal ambition, and poor supervision by top management play major roles. The ethical history or tradition of a corporation is also important, particularly the characteristics of the founder and his influence on family participation and subsequent top management. Finally, unethical behavior is likely to result if the corporate way of life results in a tendency to push too aggressively for profits. Factors external to the corporation, such as corporate financial problems, unfair practices of competitors, or the type of industry, though mentioned by some, were not major explanations for the underlying factors that lead to some corporations being unethical and others ethical.

5

THE ROLE OF TOP MANAGEMENT

In our survey, middle management was clearly of the opinion that the very nature of top management's position and its actual behavior is largely responsible for unethical or illegal corporate behavior. This was revealed, for example, in replies to an open-ended question, already discussed, relating to the differences in corporate ethics. If all first answers with respect to the role of top management were combined, one-half (53.1 percent) expressed the belief that top management is primarily responsible for the ethical or unethical behavior of a corporation, as well as for violations of government regulations. When compared with the role of a "corporate culture," over half of the respondents emphasized the role of top management one way or another, including the tendency for some corporations to select ethical (or unethical) top management personnel, particularly CEOs, to fit their patterns of doing business.

Further evidence was provided in the interviewees' responses to a more direct question as to whether top management sets the ethical tone for compliance with government laws and regulations. Nine out of ten (92.2 percent) respondents said "very much," and only 6.3 percent said "some." No one felt that top management had "little or no" influence on ethics. Some small variation by industry was found in the significant role played by top management in setting a corporation's ethical tone, and yet almost identical views were expressed about the important role of top management by those in both manufacturing and marketing.

Where corporations were generally ethical and complied with the law, this was attributed, in rank order, to a number of factors: (1)

government regulations that kept top management in line; (2) top management's explicit instructions regarding ethics and compliance with government regulations; (3) strict ethical guidelines from top management that made violations subject to dismissal; (4) requests from top management that middle management consult with them about problems in these areas; (5) middle management's respect for top management's wishes that they comply with ethical practices; (6) the importance, for ethical standards, of a history of top management continuity in leadership; and (7) the appointment to top management positions of persons from the corporate ranks. The following comments are illustrative of these and other opinions:

Top management set an example, and that is why it was a shock to middle management when the illegal Nixon campaign contributions by our corporation were revealed — *National Accounts Manager, Health Care*

*   *

Top management can change the pattern in a corporation. I worked under three vice presidents who were highly responsible, but a new one did not have the same ethical standards — *Chief Engineer, Diesel Design, Auto Industry*

*   *

Top management set the ethical tone. Government regulation, however, helped to keep top management in line — *Director, Public Relations, Foods*

*   *

Top management generally sets up the pattern for the corporation. Top management was explicit in their directives about ethics and violations. They set up audit committees within the board of directors about accounting practices and compliance with government regulations (e.g., OSHA and EEOC) — *Assistant Director, Research and Development, Soaps*

*   *

Directives came down periodically from top management on one subject or another. People thought it meant business. When a chairman of the board sends down a directive in a corporation, everyone leaps like when the President of the U.S. orders something — *Supervisor, Technical Services, Oil*

*   *

If top management got a memorandum from government, it was passed down to middle management and supervisors. Top management gave orders to comply or not to comply with the government regulations — *General Purchasing Agent, Auto Industry*

*   *

We always were hearing from top management; this we must do even though it costs plenty — *Production Process Engineer, Auto Industry*

*   *

Top management was very strong on ethics in our corporation; they put out a code of ethics and sent a letter to all middle management personnel to comply with the code or to be dismissed — *Manager, International Marketing, Chemicals*

*   *

Middle management always had an open ear to top management in making suggestions, for example, that might control unethical practices or violations of the law — *Labor Relations and Personnel Administration, Chemicals*

*   *

As long as top management had the respect of middle management, there was no problem — *Manager, Public Relations, Building Materials*

*   *

Top management set standards from the beginning of the corporation. The founders set the corporate patterns, and they are still in control. Strong ethical standards stem partly from pride in the family name — *District Manager, Sales Division, Metals*

*   *

The behavior of top management is the most successful way to get business done properly for the troops below. In our case, it was the son of the founder, e.g., a later president did not set a good ethical tone on minority relations for the corporation — *Director, Business Development, Farm Equipment*

*   *

Family-directed corporations have more effect on setting the ethical tone, particularly if the corporation name reflects the family name — *Manager, Agricultural Relations, Tires*

*   *

Top management set the whole tone of my corporation — how aggressive we would be, how much we would expand, the quality of our products, etc. The continuity of good management in our corporation was important — *Supervisor, Employee Benefit Plans, Oil*

*   *

Top management was generally succeeded by other persons of high ethical caliber, and other high standards. Therefore, there was no change in the ethics of the corporation — *Assistant Treasurer, Steel*

*   *

The fact that our corporation was highly ethical was both a combination of the history of the corporation and the selection of top management that fitted the corporation ethics. We did not go outside the corporation for top management; all of them came up from the ranks. We had some outside Board members, however — *Marketing Manager, European Division, Foods*

KNOWLEDGE OF VIOLATIONS

Further evidence of top management's role were the respondents' views that top management, should there be failures to obey the law, would generally know about these violations either before or after they occurred. Nearly three-fourths (71.9 percent) of the respondents felt that top management generally did know, 21.9 percent that they knew about some of them, and only 6.3 percent that they knew little about them. Respondents' treatment by the corporation did not significantly affect their views. Nearly two-thirds (60.3 percent) believed that, on the whole, communication to and from top management within their own corporation was good. Twice the proportion of those in marketing felt that top management usually knew about the violations, compared with those in manufacturing (84.0 percent versus 42.9 percent). It may be that the nature of sales is more visible to top management than are production problems.

They either knew at the time about violations, or sooner or later — *Cost Accountant, Special Product Division, Electrical*

*   *

Top management would know because they would have to control the expenditures necessary to prevent violations, for example, EPA and OSHA violations — *Assistant to Vice President, Marketing, Paints*

*   *

The directives to stop some violations usually came down from the top. They generally knew about the possible violations in advance because of the size of the expenditures going into preventing violations. They knew what was going on in each division each week — *Senior Process Engineer, Electrical*

*   *

Breaking the law was at the top. They used to inform personnel (e.g., top management told marketing middle management to inform buyers about the design of machines that did not exist in order to beat out the competitors). Top management was only personnel with enough "guts to violate." Middle management followed the rules imposed from above — *Systems Engineer Coordinator with Marketing, Electronics*

*   *

In the aerospace industry work, top management deals with contractual arrangements. Therefore, they know generally what is going on. They would know about falsification and waste in working out government proposals for new products, as they would about violations of government contracts — *Manager, Marketing Support, Aerospace*

*   *

Some top management would know little because they are only interested in profits, but those who came up from the ranks would know a great deal about failures to obey the law in the corporation — *Manager, Wholesale Department, Tires*

*   *

Any act that was illegally done by the corporation, top management would know about it before or as soon as it was done. Everyone each year in management had to sign a statement that we were acquainted with government rules and regulations. Sessions of middle management were held with the legal department — *Executive Vice President, International Production and Marketing, Office Machines*

*   *

The reason they would know about violations is because we had constant major operations audits rather than financial auditing generally. My job was to do this operations auditing and convey any knowledge to top management. I was not interfered with in those areas — *Systems Manager, Aerospace*

*   *

If the corporation were involved in violations, they would know about it, such as in pricefixing. In other cases they would learn what was going on, largely from auditors and quality control inspectors. We could not have done things without someone in top management's being wise to it — *Materials Manager, Light Machinery*

*   *

Communication up and down was good in my corporation, so top management would generally know of failures to obey the law — *Manager, Automotive Marketing Division, Auto Industry*

*   *

Violations of regulations would come through the influence of top management — *Marketing Manager, European Division, Foods*

*   *

It's hard to visualize that top management did not know violations were going on even if they did not know the details. Top management tended to countenance violations of middle management indirectly — *Regional Marketing Manager, Oil*

*   *

Violations were too difficult to bury. Checks and double checks from the government and competitors kept the corporation in line — *Contract Estimator, Aerospace*

A good line of communication about violations was attributed to a number of situations. For example, some department heads held frequent meetings with top management, thus enabling them to be better informed. Frequently mentioned was the use of internal operational and quality inspectors, and of financial auditors who could detect violations such as illegal marketing, payoffs, and kickbacks. In one case, a research director who was reportedly receiving kickbacks from suppliers was discovered by an internal auditor. Other checks were set up in budget supervision, plant safety inspection, and in the important matter of the legal disposal of scrap in a heavy machinery corporation.

The policy was that if anything went wrong, such as being in violation, a memo would go to top management. In fact, sometimes people in the corporation could not understand how top management found out about violations — *Manager, Employee Benefits, Auto Industry*

*   *

The lines of communication in the corporation were good. Sometimes they were too good; we felt that they often got in our hair and did not trust us in middle management — *Manager, Operations, Food*

*   *

We were always promoted from within; even top management came up from the ranks. We seldom went outside the corporation to hire anyone for middle or top management. Everyone in both middle and top management tended to know each other, and therefore knew what was going on at the top and in middle management ranks. Our plants were generally in small communities, and this helped, for local people would know what was going on if it were unethical or if it violated the law — *Manager, International Division, Steel*

On the other hand, some respondents (11.2 percent) felt that due to the size of their corporations, top management would not be involved in, or even know about, major violations. Sometimes not all top management would know; rather, only those managers in charge of certain areas like marketing, or perhaps a group vice president who dealt with several divisions or subsidiaries. As a general rule, top management would know less about violations in subsidiaries than about those in a parent corporation. One executive stated that this could explain some of the variation in violations between the parent and its subsidiaries, implying that they were greater in the latter. Others pointed out that top management did not always want to hear about violations. The possibility of government action, however, was generally important to top management and accounted for their insistence upon knowing what was going on at the middle management level. The following comments were typical of our interviewees' responses:

> Our pricefixing involvement was known by top management. As a general plant manager, I knew that things were "squeaky" in environmental violations, etc., and this was communicated to top management because there were costs involved. Otherwise, they might not know — it depends upon the individual in middle management — *General Manager, Heavy Machinery*

> *   *

> They would know about it only if the violation was of great significance. Some were reported to them, e.g., serious kickbacks — *Manager, Business Practices, Business Equipment*

> *   *

> The communication system was very good, but the size of the corporation would make it difficult for top management to know all violations — *Vice President, Marketing Division, Paper*

An attempt was also made to ascertain any differences in the types of corporate law violations about which top management would more likely know in advance, as compared with those about which they would be less likely to know. Our middle management respondents found this to be a difficult question; thus, the results should be regarded as provisional. Their own experiences with government regulations were largely limited to their own areas of operation, and for this reason they frequently found it conceptually difficult to visualize the total corporation picture referred to in this question.

Examining the total responses in order, the respondents felt that, in general, top management was most likely to know of any anti-trust violations, pricefixing infractions, possible serious plant or consumer (design) safety violations, large kickbacks, illegal foreign payoffs, and about such broad areas as violations in production quality, labor, the EPA, and tax matters. Others mentioned, although few in number, were false advertising, violations of the EEOC and warranties, and illegal entertainment, presumably of the military. Top management was less likely to know about (again in order) minor kickbacks and safety violations, price collusion at the middle management level, dealer violations (as in auto sales), poor quality production at lower levels, and labor violations — particularly at the plant, rather than at a divisional level. Still others included EEOC violations and inadequate product testing.

TOP EXECUTIVES' RESPONSIBILITY FOR CONDEMNING ILLEGAL BEHAVIOR

Overwhelming approval (92.2 percent) was expressed of the proposal that top corporate executives should speak out publicly against unethical and illegal behavior in the corporate world. This could be done through public speeches, talks at industry meetings, television interviews, and articles. A larger proportion (95.2 percent) of the manufacturing executives than of those in marketing (84.0 percent) favored top management's publicly condemning unethical corporate practices and law violations. Those who most strongly supported the view that top management should speak out were from the drug and cosmetic industries.

These views of middle management were exactly opposite to those of a small sample of top executives previously interviewed in connection with another study (Clinard and Yeager, 1980: 304). These executives, who were not retired, were of the unanimous opinion that it was not their responsibility publicly to condemn corporate illegal behavior. They felt that they did not have sufficient time to do so because of their corporate responsibilities, and furthermore, that they would be subject to severe peer group pressures were they publicly to criticize the corporate world.

In order of magnitude, the middle management executives we surveyed gave as their reasons for believing that top management has a responsibility to speak out: (1) that top management sets the tone for the industry as a whole, while no one would listen to middle management personnel; (2) that good public relations for any specific corporation, or for corporations generally, are promoted by such outspoken opinions, particularly in helping to change the public's widespread negative views of the corporate world, as expressed in public opinion polls; and (3) that business would then be better protected from such outside pressures to reform as the work of consumer protagonists like Ralph Nader. All in all, however, the feeling was that "it is better for corporations to police their own houses." Middle management generally felt that top executives should not speak out unless "their own skirts (that is, the corporation's) are clean."

> Top management should speak out generally against corporate unethical or illegal behavior. It would have an effect throughout the industry — *Director, Business Development, Farm Equipment*
>
> *   *
>
> How can corporations criticize government regulations if they condone such behavior and do nothing to correct the situation? — *Director, Research Administration, Chemicals*
>
> *   *
>
> Because it is top management's responsibility to set the tone for their industry and to speak for the industry. Top management must convince the public that industry is honest and intends to be ethical. Now there is too much adverse publicity against corporations — *Director, Corporate Service, Pharmaceuticals*
>
> *   *
>
> Providing their corporations are ethical themselves, it is their responsibility to speak out — *District Sales Manager, Steel*
>
> *   *
>
> The only way we can sell our free enterprise system is for business to let people know what it is all about by speaking out against

unethical practices. People now think that the system is crooked. We cannot stonewall the corporate system as Nixon did. — *Plant Manager, Chemicals*

*   *

Corporations should do everything they can to police themselves, and it might help to get the government off their backs if top management spoke out. This would give a better public image; the corporations now have a poor public image — *Supervisor, Employee Benefit Plans, Oil*

*   *

It would improve public opinion about the corporate world, which at the present time is quite negative — *Cost Accountant, Special Products Division, Electrical*

*   *

American industry has a bad reputation among the general public, and it would help. If industry occasionally knocked itself, it would be in better shape with the public — *National Accounts Manager, Health Care*

*   *

I have always thought that industry was lax in these things. Business is always trying to present a favorable image, and actually they have a hell of an image with the public. Business should speak out against unethical and illegal practices rather than have others do it — *Materials Manager, Light Machinery*

*   *

Business and corporate top management have a bad reputation with the public; to stand up and admit unethical practices and violations would show what we in corporate business really believe in — *Executive Vice President, International Production and Marketing, Business Machines*

*   *

I believe that it is up to top management to get the rest of the corporations to be honest. The public would see that industry is for honesty; now the public has a feeling that industry is only after money and is dishonest — *Manager, Operations, Foods*

*   *

Absolutely. Leaders of the corporate world establish the ethical standards under which we operate and the climate of how you compete. Business is what America's all about — *Manager, Business Practices, Business Equipment*

*   *

Ethics must be preached by the men (top management) in the pulpit — *Division Sales Manager, Oil*

*   *

They should damned well educate the public about what the corporate world is really like. They should speak out when it is unethical and things are wrong, and also when they are right — *General Manager, Heavy Machinery*

*   *

If top management spoke out, we would not need pressure from guys like Nader or even the government — *Production Process Engineer, Auto Industry*

*   *

The situation would be handled better than by Ralph Nader. The corporate world still must have certain government regulations — *Production Director, Tires*

*   *

I never succeeded in getting any of top management to speak out. They did not like to make public appearances on the question. They should mainly speak to universities. For top management to speak out would do much to change the negative views about corporations, particularly held by university students — *General Counsel, Foods*

The few who were opposed to top management's speaking out believed that (1) it is not their responsibility to do so; (2) it is difficult for them to do so because of their heavy corporate responsibilities; (3) some top management executives are not good public spokesmen; and (4) it represents, basically, taking "cheap shots" at someone else — that is, other corporations. They believed that a corporation should keep its own house in order and let other corporations take charge of their own, without comments from outsiders.

On the other hand, middle management took a completely opposite view toward top executives' condemnation of the flagrantly unethical and illegal behavior of a specifically named corporation. Three out of four of them (76.7 percent) replied with a definite "No." They gave several reasons for not speaking out: (1) it would be too specific in nature; (2) it is the responsibility of government to deal with individual cases, not theirs; (3) nothing would be gained by this action; (4) it might lead to libel suits against them; (5) the executives might not know the true facts of the case; (6) their own corporation's profits might be indirectly affected because of possible retaliation from other corporations; (7) many might think that there were ulterior motives in such specific attacks, as for example attempts to undermine the financial strength of the other corporation; (8) no corporation is completely "clean" ethically or legally, and one should not "go against the rules of the corporate game"; and (9) specific situations can be corrected by other means, including industry associations. Top management also appears to feel the same way, as shown in the study of the opinions of many among the Fortune 500 corporations:

> There is great reluctance among business executives to "name names" or publicly criticize other businesses for illegal actions — whether because of fear of a loss of business, concern about "washing our dirty linen in public," anxiety about being "kicked out of the club," or loathness to claim moral superiority and the right to censure others. Yet there is recognition that businessmen's silence on the transgressions of other businesses has contributed to a general public belief that "they're all alike" or "they're all in this together" [Silk and Vogel, 1976: 227].

The minority of middle management executives felt that top management should also speak out about specific corporations, that it was their duty to do so, and that it would improve the public image of all corporations. Others felt that they should speak out, but only in cases involving competitors. One executive in the aircraft manufacturing industry favored the proposal, with the exception that "they should not speak out against anyone in the aluminum industry," who were obviously their suppliers.

ATTITUDES TOWARD TOP MANAGEMENT COMPENSATION

In view of their statements that top management plays a major role in unethical and illegal corporate behavior, it might be presumed that our respondents' opinions may well reflect a certain resentment, even jealousy, toward top management, due largely to the marked differentials between top and middle management with respect to salaries, bonuses, stock options, and various "perks" (Compensation Review, 1976; McKean and Monsen, 1975; Clinard and Yeager, 1980: 231, 275-276). Top management personnel of large corporations, particularly the CEOs, receive salaries that can well exceed $200,000, $500,000, or even $1 million, and retirement severance pay can run into six figures or more. For example, the chairman of the board and the president of the Savin Corporation were reported to have received severance payments totaling $4,250,000 (The Wall Street Journal, March 26, 1982). U.S. Secretary of Commerce Malcolm Baldridge received $1,274,890 in incentive, severance, and pension payments when he resigned as chairman of the board to join the Reagan administration. He has stated that these payments were in line with "common business practice" (The Wall Street Journal, June 3, 1981). In addition, top management personnel often receive noncash compensation or corporate luxuries in the form of "perks." These noncash benefits often include the free use of corporation limousines, airplanes, yachts, and lodges, as well as memberships in exclusive city and country clubs. Their offices are often huge, with a relaxed living room/library atmosphere, and frequently equipped with fireplaces, private bathrooms, oriental carpets, a wall covered wtih fine art objects and, if the executive is really powerful, an adjacent private dining room. Many chief executives even operate in a push-button atmosphere, opening and closing draperies and doors by remote control. One top executive recalled that an important sign of status was "the amount of greenery an office had; the more plants, the more power" (The Wall Street Journal, January 15, 1982).

Replies by middle management executives to questions about this particular issue of compensation and "perks" did not indicate an overall resentment of this differential treatment. Nearly half of them (44.4 percent) expressed little or no resentment, and 31.7 percent said that they had felt only "some." A partial relationship was noted between their treatment by the corporation and their resentment of top management's compensation. Those who felt that they had been treated only "fairly well" had a statistically significant negative view of top management's high compensation, though no significant difference was found by length of retirement. Less resentment was found among middle management executives in manufacturing (43.2 percent) than among those in marketing (52.0 percent). As noted earlier, respondents with only a high school education showed the lowest resentment of top management's greater compensation. Their high compensation was least resented by those from the drugs and cosmetics and in the motor vehicle industries; it was most resented by those from the aerospace, metals, and food and beverage industries.

One-third (34.4 percent) of the total respondents felt that had they been in the position of the top management executives, they would have wanted what these executives were receiving; in fact, they believe that these financial benefits create goals for which middle management strives. Other reasons were that with a high percentage of their salaries paid out in taxes, the differences are not as great as they appear. Furthermore, top management people deserve higher pay because of their heavy corporate responsibilities, the great competitive demand for competent managers, particularly CEOs, the often limited tenure of CEOs and others at the very "top," and because these "top" salaries represent only a small fraction of the total corporate expenditures.

> Some middle management may resent the high salaries and the bonuses paid to top management, but most feel that top management earns every cent of it. They are married not to their wives but to the corporate jobs. They are worth that amount of money. Their salaries are actually minimal in terms of the total cash flow of the corporation. Moreover, there are not many really capable CEOs available — *Assistant Superintendent, Oil*

> *   *

> Most middle management feels that top management has to put in many more hours and has greater responsibilities. A top management person has so little time to himself; his time must go to the corporation. With high taxes their income may not be as great as it looks. Top management does not generally have a long tenure, either — *Director, Engineering, Chemicals*

> *   *

> Those fellows in top management have no time to lead their own lives. They have power, but they must have sacrificed a great deal

to get it. As middle management, moreover, you would like to be in their position — *Manager, International Division, Steel*

*   *

Some day you might be there. No one is worth that much, but the majority have the ability — *District Sales Manager, Chemicals*

*   *

Middle management is striving to get up there also. The burden on top management is so great that few begrudge them their salaries, perks, etc. They have the ability — *Manager, Business Practices, Business Equipment*

*   *

Top management has great responsibility. It takes a physical toll — often top management executives do not live long in retirement — *Assistant Treasurer, Steel*

*   *

If I got there, I would want the same high salaries and perks — *Manager, Automotive Marketing Division, Auto Industry*

*   *

I have always felt the man who is capable of attaining and holding a position of chairman of the board is entitled to the pay he receives — *Manager, Western Division, Marketing, Appliances*

*   *

The tax structure takes a lot of earnings of top management. If it were not for this fact I definitely think that the salaries are too high. Top management deserves something, but not that much — *Associate Director, Research and Development, Soaps*

*   *

I think that they are entitled to their high salaries and perks. They are selected because they are the best available people — *Sales Manager, Parts Division, Business Machines*

*   *

This causes envy rather than resentment. It is a goal that you can strive for — to receive their salaries and benefits. Top management is justified in terms of the large size of the corporations they run. I aspired to top management — *Manager, Advanced Engineering Facilities, Automotive and Nuclear Parts*

*   *

If they could get top management, such as a CEO, for less, why don't they? Top management has a tougher life compared to middle management — *Marketing Manager, European Division, Foods*

*   *

I never expected to be in top management. They earn what they get; their direction must have made the corporation pretty profitable or they would not have gotten their high salaries — *Advanced Design Engineer, Auto Industry*

*   *

Their salaries, etc., are a very small percentage of the total corporate budget. It is a part of the American dream to achieve this level. If you think you can do it, just try to do it. It is very tough to do their jobs, and competition for them is very, very great — *Manager, International Government Relations, Oil*

*   *

It makes for an unholy ambition by some middle management to get there by any means — *Director, Corporate Taxes, Chemicals*

On the other hand, only one out of four (23.8 percent) believed that middle management greatly resented this differentiation in compensation. The respondents who did express strong resentment said that top management personnel have excessively high salaries and that the compensation differential is far too great, particularly in light of their feelings that middle management must bear the brunt of the real corporate work responsibilities. According to some respondents, the high salaries of top management are voted by the inner clique of a corporation's boards of directors. The members of this upper echelon look after themselves; they do not necessarily reduce their own salaries and other benefits when profits decline, while middle management salaries are based on the standards of performance.

If there were a more equitable distribution of profits it would prevent some middle management and on down the line from receiving kickbacks, etc. — *Plant Manager, Aluminum*

*   *

Top management is often regarded as a little group at the top looking out for themselves. If top management can turn around a corporation, it is probably worth it. There is a tendency, however, to increase top management benefits even if there has been no increase in profits — *Supervisor, Employee Benefit Plans, Oil*

*   *

The differential does bother middle management. Many middle managers think that top management has made their salary decisions themselves. I do not think that top management generally is worth that much difference — *Labor Relations and Personnel Administration, Chemicals*

*   *

Top management constitutes a "private club." They protect each other. Their salaries, etc., are not based on profits — *Plant Manager, Aluminum*

*   *

They get too much. They do not earn it. Even when responsibilities are diminished they get the same salary. Middle management resents these high salaries. What man is worth $20,000 a week? They do not really make decisions alone anyway — they usually have advisors. The salaries, etc., are not tied much to corporation losses — *Executive Vice President, Foods*

*   *

Everyone in middle management generally is underpaid. I wonder, though, whether the differential between middle and top management should be that great. It is counterbalanced somewhat if middle management is taken care of in some way such as by bonuses. The CEO is worth it to a certain extent — he is the image, the goal setter, and he provides leadership for a corporation. If you do not have a good leader you are a dead corporation — *Plant Manager, Chemicals*

*   *

It is a serious inequality. It's not salaries so much as extras, such as stock bonuses. One can only guess as to whether they have that much ability. They are overpaid. Against the total income of the large corporations, however, top management salaries, etc., are not so much of an expenditure — *Senior Process Engineer, Electrical*

*   *

Middle management feels that top management is not that much "smarter" than they are — *Director, Business Development, Toiletries*

*   *

Here I am a middle management person doing all of the work. Top management is more in an advisory capacity. Just because a company is making money does not mean that top management is doing that much — *General Purchasing Agent, Auto Industry*

*   *

Middle management generally resents the salaries and the perks of top management. I once recommended to the board of directors that they cut top salaries by 10 percent. I was as popular as a "skunk." Later they did not give me salary increases. Top management salaries are overdone, and their effects upon other employees are quite great. They become symbolic of the status of top management all the way down the line, and it sets up a caste system within the corporation — *General Counsel, Foods*

In conclusion, an overwhelming nine out of ten middle management executives felt that top management sets the ethical tone of the corporation. Nearly three-fourths felt that top management usually knew about law violations either before, or not long after, they occurred. Because of their influence and the important role top management plays, nine out of ten felt that top corporate executives should speak out publicly against the unethical and illegal behavior within the corporate world. Obviously, these strong negative views could simply represent jealousy of top management or an attitude of "sour grapes" because they, in middle management, had not reached the highest corporate echelons. This did not seem to be the case, for when questioned about the much higher compensation of top management, nearly half expressed little or no resentment, and one-third felt only some resentment. It may be concluded, then, that middle management's views of the role of top management, in relation to corporate unethical behavior and law violations, are likely to have been unaffected by their own positions within the corporation.

6

PRESSURES ON MIDDLE MANAGEMENT

TYPES OF PRESSURES

The executives discussed in great detail the pressures under which middle management personnel regularly work. The question they were asked was phrased to cover the types of pressures they themselves found in their work, those they noticed in other positions within their corporations, as well as among persons holding similar posts in other corporations; in other words, they were asked to respond in broad terms. Their replies totaled 258, an average of 4.0 answers per person and specifying seventeen types of pressures.

In terms of *total* responses, the greatest pressure (21.7 percent) was to show profits and to keep costs in line (see Table 6.1). This was followed by time pressures (15.1 percent) and production and sales quotas (9.7 percent). Other pressures were related to the maintenance of satisfactory employee relations (8.1 percent) and corporate "politics," including relations with top management. When the analysis was confined to their *first* response, these had a slightly different order; the pressure of time was mentioned first (34.9 percent), followed by that to show profits and keep costs in line (28.6 percent).

PRESSURES AFFECTING PERSONAL LIFE

Middle management executives exhibited a varied capacity to deal personally with corporate pressures. Slightly more than half (53.3

TABLE 6.1   Pressures on Middle Management*

Type of Pressure	Responses	Percentage
Pressures to show profits and keep costs in line	56	21.7
Time pressures	39	15.1
Production and sales quotas	25	9.7
Employee relations	21	8.1
Pressures to meet quality standards	16	6.2
Union pressures	14	5.4
Product development	11	4.3
Upward promotion pressures	7	2.7
Pressures to do things that are unethical	6	2.3
Corporate politics — relations with top management	15	5.8
Dealing with local government and government regulations	6	2.3
Employee safety pressures	5	1.9
Corporate politics — relations with press	5	1.9
Finding right employee for the job	4	1.6
Pressures to satisfy customers	3	1.2
Balance work and family	3	1.2
Others	20	7.8
Total	258	100.0

*Total responses.

percent) thought that their marriages had been adversely affected by the pressures under which they worked. They indicated that this had been due largely to their frequent and often lengthy absences from home, sometimes for a total of several months each year, and to the changes of location necessitated by their corporate assignments. Others said that their wives believed they worked too hard, frequently having to take work home. One said he would sometimes even have to leave a dinner party in order to complete some important work. Two executives said that they always put their business responsibilities ahead of their families' needs. On the other hand, nearly half of the sample (47.7 percent) said that neither their marriages nor their family life had been affected by the severity of the corporate pressures under which they worked. Several, in fact, stated that their wives and children were very understanding about the pressures under which they worked.

I worked 39 years and never missed a day's work. I put the corporation ahead of my family — *Production Director, Tires*

*   *

My wife thought that I worked too hard. It was the pattern of corporate life — *Executive Vice President, Foods*

*   *

I had frequent headaches due to tensions. My wife objected to my staying away from home, working on weekends and traveling — *Advanced Design Engineer, Auto Industry*

*   *

It was rough on my wife, my being away from home and the children so much. You must have an understanding wife if you work for a corporation — *Director, Engineering, Chemicals*

*   *

I traveled all over the United States for twenty-five years, but my wife and four children understood. Corporate transfers were difficult for them, however — *National Accounts Manager, Health Care*

*   *

No health problems. I traveled a lot, but it did not affect my family life. In fact, corporate life gave our family many perks that they would otherwise not have had — *Manager, International Marketing, Chemicals*

*   *

I moved to various new assignments; I lived in 18 different places. The children were raised primarily by my wife; they went to many different schools. Middle management pressures resulted in my getting heart trouble. So I took early retirement — *Regional Marketing Manager, Oil*

The respondents also discussed the effects of these corporate pressures on their own health. Many of them believed that such pressures had greatly affected their health; less than half of them (45.5 percent) said that they had no health problems. Of the remainder, 25.5 percent had had some general health problems, principally high blood pressure, and many (16.4 percent) had ulcers. Heart trouble affected 7.3 percent, and 5.5 percent had had to take early retirement due to various health problems.

I developed high blood pressure. My wife was happy when I retired. She said, "Now we can have some fun" — *Manager, Automotive Marketing Division, Auto Industry*

*   *

I tried to adjust to the pressures without resulting long-term damages, e.g., on business trips I took along a bowling ball. Many of my friends died under these pressures, e.g., they had heart attacks — *General Purchasing Agent, Auto Industry*

*   *

I had to move 33 times. It affected my marriage to a certain extent in not being home enough with the children, etc. Had ulcers and high blood pressure — *Manager, Western Division, Marketing, Appliances*

*   *

I used to have violent headaches due to pressures, but probably this is why I never got ulcers — *Sales Manager, Parts Division, Business Machines*

*   *

I had ulcers for 30 years. It was part of the job — *Marketing Manager, European Division, Foods*

*   *

Pressures eventually amounted to too much according to my doctor, who said that I would have either a heart attack or a stroke. So I retired — *Plant Manager, Auto Parts*

*   *

I had high blood pressure. The family suffered by my attendance at many meetings and being away from home a lot. We had corporate dinner meetings and other meetings. We had a lot of family fights as a result — *Assistant to Vice President, Marketing Division, Paint*

*   *

I had high blood pressure, and in fact, I had to take early retirement. It was because of corporation pressures and top corporation officials being changed, which was upsetting to me — *General Divisions Manager, Heavy Machinery*

* *

I had ulcers. Part of it was my inability to understand what my superiors wanted — *Labor Relations and Personnel Administrator, Chemicals*

PRESSURES AND UNETHICAL AND ILLEGAL BEHAVIOR

Work pressures on these middle management respondents set the stage for measuring their feelings about the relation of such pressures to unethical and illegal corporate behavior. Nine out of ten (90.6 percent) said that they felt such pressures do lead to unethical behavior within a corporation. Almost one-fourth (23.4 percent) reported that there was a great deal of pressure that could lead to such behavior. No significant statistical difference was found between their views of their own treatment by the corporation and their estimates of the relation of work pressures to unethical behavior by middle management executives.

Practically no difference was noted in the proportion of those in manufacturing and in marketing who felt that excessive pressures were exerted on middle management. The executives who were most likely to believe that pressures on middle management did contribute to unethical behavior were from the fields of industrial and farm equipment, aerospace technology, and food and beverages; those who believed that pressures had the least effect were from the oil and chemical industries.

Middle management works under terrific pressures. You take an aerospace program that has great pressures on middle management. It can lead to divorces, alcoholism, "pill popping" for ulcers, and the use of tranquilizers. Under these conditions middle management is willing to do almost anything — *Manager, Systems Management, Aerospace*

* *

You get the pressure so strong from top management that you will make judgmental efforts to make things come out right even if you have to use unethical practices such as lying about production or marketing progress. The pressures can result in cutting corners, e.g., on quality; a corporation has got to be a going concern — *Division Manager, Machinery*

*   *

You start out of college with high ideals and due to pressures these ideals deteriorate during one's corporate experience. Middle management violates their ethics, mainly to get the job done — *Director, Corporate Taxes, Chemicals*

*   *

Pressures force some to sweep things that might be unethical under the rug — *Budget Coordinator, Aerospace*

*   *

I know of a case of a man who went into quality control inspection, and he quit because of pressures to put out an inaccurate quality report that top management wanted — *Manager, Recording Development, Records*

*   *

Even if it requires practices that are unethical, middle management has to try to meet a corporation's objective, as for example, a sales quota — *Division Sales Manager, Oil*

*   *

Some middle management were forced, for example, to deal unethically with labor problems that interfered with production — *Manager, Manufacturing Facility Planning, Farm Equipment*

*   *

In the tire business, for example, a person in middle management marketing might be tempted to oversell or to overstock a dealer to show a good performance to top management — *Manager, Wholesale Department, Tires*

*   *

Particularly there are pressures in meeting time schedules in manufacturing. This often results in cutting corners or falsifying reports. If, for example, the production schedule was exceeded in a given month, middle management would carry over the difference to the next — *Manager, Advanced Engineering Facilities, Nuclear Parts*

*   *

There are pressures on middle management to get a favorable deal for the corporation, particularly in labor contracts, or with foreign governments, and this can lead to unethical behavior — *General Counsel, Foods*

*   *

In order to meet cost limitations, the quality of the work might be reduced, such as deliberately missing a few things that were supposed to be done in auto assembly work. This pressure to keep down costs affects auto recalls — *Division Chief Engineer, Diesel Design, Auto Industry*

*   *

If those in middle management "cannot cut the mustard," they will cut corners — drop the quality and change the material. For example, we were making metal bolts of expensive material and we found that someone else in middle management had made them of inferior material so he would not get into trouble over exceeding his budget — *General Manager, Heavy Machinery*

*   *

Pressures can lead to middle management forging fake orders that go on the books and then are later taken off the books. This made the sales in a given month look good — *Systems Engineer Coordinator with Marketing, Electronics*

*   *

I have heard people talk in other companies about being unethical in order to maintain middle management's position or to look good for salary increases or promotions — *Factory Manager, Heavy Machinery*

*   *

It largely depends upon the ethics of the person; some middle management can resist pressures and others cannot — *Cost Accountant, Special Products Division, Electrical*

*   *

I do not see how pressures affect ethics. Pressures are a part of your job — *Supervisor, Technical Services, Oil*

*   *

People who will do unethical things will do them whether there is pressure or not. They would cheat in golf or in anything else — *National Accounts Manager, Health Care*

A smaller, but still sizable, proportion (in fact, three-fourths or 78.2 percent) thought that pressures led to the commission of illegal acts by middle management. Most felt that pressures led to some, but not a great deal, of this type of behavior (68.8 percent versus 9.4 percent). Statistically, there was no relation between corporate treatment of them and their views about pressures being conducive to violations. Length of retirement also played no statistically significant role in their responses.

Two-thirds of the executives in both manufacturing and in marketing believed that some pressures did lead to the commission of illegal acts. This belief was most often held by those from the aerospace and the electric and appliance industries; least likely to hold such beliefs were metal industry executives.

Three further conclusions may be drawn. First, these pressures are not always a sufficient and necessary cause for all violations. Some respondents pointed out, for example, that the real effects of pressures depended on the specific manner in which top management dealt with middle management and the degree of open communication that existed between the two levels. They mentioned also that much depended on the personal integrity of the individual middle manager. Other respondents pointed out that the realization of their being under top management pressure can be used by some executives as an excuse for unethical behavior. Second, the pressures are more likely to lead to unethical behavior than to actual violations of the law. In their comments, in fact, nearly one out of five drew a sharp distinction between the two; others disagreed, feeling that the line between corporate ethics and law violations is too fine. Third, their general support for government regulations may reflect, in part, middle management's general feeling that they are powerless in the face of pressures from

top management and that government intervention is therefore necessary to control corporate conduct. The following excerpts are typical of
respondents' views about the relation of pressure to unethical practices:

Law violations are about the same as ethics, except in the former
you go to jail — *Director, Business Development, Toiletries*

*   *

Normally pressures would not lead to violations, but it could, by
sneaking material by a government inspector. (I built equipment
for nuclear submarines) — *Manager, Advanced Engineering
Facilities, Automotive and Nuclear Parts*

*   *

Pressures may result in cost-plus government contract padding —
Contract Estimator, Aerospace

*   *

For example, middle management is often pushed to make a profit
by "screwing the government," and by conducting unethical or
illegal relationships with the union — *Plant Manager, Chemicals*

*   *

Pressures might lead middle management to do a slipshod job,
saying, "I do not give a damn because of the pressures," either in
quality or in complying with government regulations — *Assistant
to Vice President, Manufacturing Division, Paints*

*   *

Pressures can force carelessness in obeying the law. I get sloppy
under pressure; also I get ulcers — *Production Process Engineer,
Auto Industry*

*   *

Pressures on middle management may result in cutting corners
(e.g., proper maintenance of equipment, which can result in violations of government regulations). The pressure to perform can
really crack a guy up and he will not use his proper judgment about
obeying ethics or the law — *Division Manager, Machinery*

*   *

Pressures carry over from ethics to violations to save time or money in getting the job done (e.g., not taking care of a safety violation or falsifying weight on scrap sales, etc.). Sometimes law violations can come from job dissatisfaction such as lack of proper recognition by top management — *Assistant to Vice President, Manufacturing, Paints*

*   *

Middle management will tend to get involved in OSHA safety violations if their budget is short. Also, violations can occur particularly in meeting government contract delivery dates. This pressure on middle management comes from top management and the government. If delivery dates are not met, the corporation will be charged a late fee. Middle management therefore may loosen up on the quality of the product with no, or little, inspection — *General Purchasing Agent, Auto Industry*

*   *

Law violations depend upon the degree of top management pressures and the ethics of top management — *Director, Public Relations, Foods*

*   *

Pressures have more effect on ethics than on violations. Violations of government regulations in our industry risked losing future government contracts, which is a difficult situation. Our corporation wanted to avoid bad publicity, for example, on OSHA violations — *Manager, Systems Management, Aerospace*

*   *

Pressures result mostly in unethical practices, but not illegal — *Manager, Manufacturing Facility Planning, Farm Equipment*

*   *

It is up to the individual's own ethics whether he violates government regulations because of pressures — *Production Manager, Paper*

PRESSURES AND INDIVIDUAL ETHICS

So far, it has been indicated that middle management executives feel that (1) pressures on their group are extensive and serious; (2)

these pressures, in the judgment of the majority of the respondents, may lead to unethical behavior and law violations; (3) top management has a great deal to do with exerting undue pressures that might result in unethical or illegal behavior; and (4) corporate pressures affected the personal lives of a large proportion of them.

One might expect, based on these views, that many respondents in the sample would report that they had also experienced undue pressure to violate their own personal ethical standards. This was not the case: Three-fourths (74.6 percent) said that no pressures had been put on them, and if one adds the 15.9 percent who reported only a little pressure, the total with none or few pressures reaches 90.5 percent of the total sample. Thus, only 10.9 percent (or seven cases) personally experienced either some or much pressure. The following comments were made by six of the seven respondents who admitted personal involvement:

I had a boss who wanted me to join his church, and I complained to his supervisor about his religious proselytizing — *Electrical*

*   *

At times I did have pressures exerted on me for excessive sales quotas — *Steel*

*   *

I had to testify in a pricefixing case involving top management, and pressures were put on me as to what to say — *Health Care*

*   *

Pressures were put on me to make political contributions that would be in the interest of the corporation — *Business Equipment*

*   *

They put pressures on me at the divisional level for sales, so I put excessive sales pressures on our dealers — *Tires*

*   *

I usually got enough gifts from suppliers to fill the bedroom. I gave them all away — *Auto Industry*

To explain the low incidence of reported personal unethical or illegal behavior, one can assume four possibilities: (1) the pressures put on them personally were of a different nature than most middle management executives experienced; (2) the actual incidence of such situations would be statistically small in any event, in a sample totaling only 64 respondents; (3) the sample consisted of extremely ethical persons who were able to resist pressures; and/or (4) they did not want to admit, or they failed to recall, any unethical incidents that had occurred. One executive said that he tried to "remember only positive things." It is not unusual to find that persons respond one way to a question that applies to others and in an entirely different manner to one that relates to direct, personal involvement. This is especially true in a personal interview situation; a somewhat different response might have been given had they been responding to an impersonal, mailed questionnaire, provided that their answers were frank and that they had reflected more carefully on the question. For example, in a study of the views of prison guards of inmates and inmates of guards, Wheeler (1961) found that each group had a generally negative attitude toward the other when asked what other guards or inmates thought. On the other hand, when asked their own opinions of inmates or guards, they had more positive and more individualized views of each other.

7

GOVERNMENT REGULATION

A large proportion of the executives felt that the presence of government regulation does not in itself lead to a negative atmosphere conducive to violations. More than half (56.3 percent) took the position that government regulation produces little or no negative effect. In more detail, 17.2 percent said "no effect," 39.1 percent felt "a little," 28.1 percent said "much," and only 15.6 percent thought government regulations had "very much effect." No statistically significant relation was found between their opinions and the length of their retirement. Almost identical views about the role of government regulations were expressed by those in manufacturing and in marketing. Executives from the drug and cosmetic industries believed the most strongly that government regulation does not contribute to violations, while aerospace and industrial, as well as farm equipment executives, believed the most strongly that regulation does have a negative effect.

Some pointed out that even difficulties in complying with one government regulation do not necessarily produce an attitude of non-compliance with others. Others added that government regulation is needed to assure worker and consumer safety, for example, and to promote ethical behavior by others within the industry. Some of these regulations had originally been necessitated, in fact, by unethical industry practices. Such general views are illustrated by the following comments:

> There is a great deal of antagonism to government regulations, but in itself this does not contribute to violations of government regulations — *Division Manager, Machinery*

*   *

In certain industries, such as the chemical industry, it is important
to have essential government regulations (for example, worker
and consumer safety). This does not lead to antagonism to
government regulations as a whole — *Supervisor, Employee Benefit Plans, Chemicals*

*   *

We need to have government regulations to control the industry.
All corporations then know that others are operating under them
also — *Contract Estimator, Aerospace*

*   *

Government restrictions are often well conceived and are necessary (e.g., Robinson-Patman Act and Anti-Trust) — *District Sales
Manager, Steel*

*   *

Some laws and regulations are very good even with the burden
imposed on the corporations. Regulations help make the industry
competitive — *Manager, Business Practices, Business Equipment*

*   *

A rigid set of government rules does not lead to violations. Responsible corporate management would see to it that there were
few violations. An irresponsible corporation might be affected by
a general negative attitude to government regulations — *Director,
Research Administration, Chemicals*

*   *

We may not agree with regulations (for example, emissions,
mileage, safety, etc.) but this does not mean that there will be
violations of regulations — *Division Chief, Diesel Design, Auto
Industry*

*   *

Just the opposite. Government regulations frighten corporations
into being good citizens — *Director, Business Development, Toiletries*

*   *

All complain about government regulations, but this is not the reason for their violation. Government regulations are often a burden, but they do not constitute in themselves an ethical problem — *General Counsel, Foods*

                    *   *

It depends upon what government regulations, such as safety and pollution regulations, that are needed. But if government regulations are unnecessary they can cause people to violate them, due to a generally negative attitude that develops toward the government — *Cost Accountant, Special Production Division, Electrical*

                    *   *

Some of the government regulations were brought on by unethical practices within the industry — *Director, Public Relations, Foods*

                    *   *

Obligations to comply with the law do not result in antagonisms to government in spite of all the talk. It may cost them money, but that is a different problem — *Assistant Director, Research and Development, Soaps*

On the other hand, those who expressed the view that government regulation does contribute to a negative attitude toward government in general gave these reasons, in order of magnitude: (1) the presence of too many regulations produces negative attitudes; (2) the lack of government familiarity with corporate problems brings about negative attitudes toward them; (3) many regulations are too complex for a thorough understanding; and (4) the unrealistic and unfair nature of the regulations leads to the development of negative attitudes. Some interviewees pointed out that the negative effects of regulations are caused, in part, by the fact that the persons responsible for writing them (and also enforcing them) were often largely uninformed about the manifold facets of the industry. In such a setting, a generally negative attitude toward government is fostered, thus endangering compliance with regulations as a whole.

People who establish regulations often do not know about the steel industry. The image of government is not good, and there is a general negative reaction when regulations are too trivial and not fair — *General Manager, Marketing, Steel*

*   *

Regulations often produce an atmosphere unfavorable to government. Government inspectors should be those who have worked in a plant previously — *Senior Process Engineer, Electrical*

*   *

Government gets in our hair. Many government officials do not know how to run a business. This builds up a negative attitude toward the government in general and it can contribute to violations — *Manager, Operations, Foods*

*   *

The pressure of government regulations has caused many corporations to abandon their responsibility — *Regional Marketing Manager, Oil*

*   *

You get so damned weary reading regulations that you try to find ways of getting around them and getting something accomplished. Under pressure there is a tendency to violate a strict rule — *Director, Engineering, Chemicals*

*   *

Government regulation foments disrespect for the law. It results in an attitude towards government that you should get away with as much as you can. The judgment on whether you violate is based on what the penalties would be if you get caught — *Manager, Public Relations, Building Materials*

*   *

Some regulations are so asinine and costly that they result in negativism toward government and thus their violation. Middle management says: "So what the hell; they are crazy fools in the government." There is, as a result, much discretion in middle management and top management as to whether a regulation is really important or not — *Manager, Management Systems, Aerospace*

*   *

It is a major factor because (1) many do not understand the regulations, or (2) they think that many of them are unfair. And if it is the latter they will violate the hell out of it instead of trying to get it changed — *Operations Manager, Tires*

*   *

Top management uses government regulations as a soapbox. I was in international corporate business — compared to other countries we have less regulation of business. It should not be an excuse for violating regulations, but they do use it — *Executive Vice President, International Production and Marketing, Business Machines*

INDUSTRY SELF-REGULATION

Each respondent was asked: "What do you see as an alternative to government regulations: Can industry police itself?" A somewhat surprising majority (57.2 percent) of the 63 executives who answered this question replied that government is needed and that industry cannot police itself. If one adds the responses that even with industry help, some government regulation is necessary (14.1 percent), the total who felt that various degrees of government regulation are required was nearly three out of four (71.5 percent). There was no statistically significant relation between the responses and length of retirement.

The following reasons were given for industry's inability to regulate itself: (1) the unethical behavior of some top management personnel and some corporations within an industry make government regulation necessary; (2) the greed of some corporations, and the differences in competitive practices, make regulation advisable, if not obligatory; and (3) self-regulatory measures cannot be enforced. Some comments:

In general, industries cannot police themselves without governmental regulations. Some corporations are honest and others are dishonest — *Manager, Operations, Marketing, Food*

*   *

We must have someone to moderate industry. Some form of centralized control through government is necessary — *District Sales Manager, Chemicals*

*   *

Industry is primarily interested in short-run profits, and management people in their own personal advancement. Even the most ethical corporations would be less ethical if they were not regulated by government — *Director, Business Development, Toiletries*

*   *

I do not have that much faith in people and certain corporations; there are always a few crooks among us — *Director, Corporate Services, Pharmaceuticals*

*   *

Industry can regulate itself if it is dedicated, but it is not. Government has come in because industry had not done it — chemicals, water pollution, strip mining. Industry has learned to do things right because of government regulation. Without regulation the bad situations would come back — *General Manager, Marketing, Steel*

*   *

I do not think that any industry can regulate itself. In spite of all the complaints from business, government tends to keep the industry in line. I would not like to see the "dog eat dog" situation that would develop if there were not some overseeing of activities of industry by the government. Particularly it would be difficult for the smaller corporations — *Manager, Manufacturing Facility Planning, Farm Equipment*

*   *

There are too many unethical top management people in corporate business so the industry cannot regulate itself. So, as much as I despise the government, we must keep some limited government regulations — *Manager, Operations, Foods*

*   *

Not completely. We must have some strong guidelines. If there are not regulations, there are enough corporations that are borderline that would take advantage of the situation. Without government regulation, corporations would bring out defective or unsafe products — *Manager, Advanced Engineering Facilities, Automotive and Nuclear Parts*

*　　　　　　　　　　　*

Industry cannot regulate itself. There must be a certain amount of Big Brother in our country or we would have anarchy — *Manager, Sales, Parts Division, Business Machines*

*　　　　　　　　　　　*

Industry is incapable of regulating itself because of competition. If one corporation starts to cheat, the rest will follow — *General Counsel, Foods*

*　　　　　　　　　　　*

Cannot police own industry because not every corporate person (in top management) is ethical, and never will be — *Manager, Marketing, Western Division, Appliances*

*　　　　　　　　　　　*

I do not think that an industry can police itself. Perhaps it is because I always worked under government regulations and, therefore, I consider them to be necessary — *District Sales Manager, Steel*

*　　　　　　　　　　　*

A lot of industry will not put extra capital into many important safety or pollution areas unless forced to do so by government — *Production Director, Tires*

*　　　　　　　　　　　*

The aerospace industry never has been able to regulate itself. Government has had to regulate it, particularly regarding safety — *Contract Estimator, Aerospace*

*　　　　　　　　　　　*

Without government regulation there would be many unsafe and defective products. What Nader started has had its positive effects. The auto industry can no more police itself than the petroleum industry. Government has to set standards to encourage industry to be more responsible — *Director, Business Development, Farm Equipment*

*   *

Without government regulations, corporations' dishonest top management people would continue to do what they do without its being illegal — *Cost Accountant, Special Products Division, Electrical*

*   *

I doubt if industry can do it. A lot of things they now have to do because of government regulations they would omit and retain the additional profits — *Manager, National Accounts, Health Care*

*   *

Got to have government. The industry proposals for self-regulation that I was in were ineffective — no way that they can be enforced. Corporations will not respect industry agreements — *Manager, Public Relations, Building Materials*

*   *

Unfortunately, industry cannot regulate itself, although they should. Practically all industries have some quality problems that government regulations protect — *Supervisor, Employee Benefits, Oil*

*   *

We need some government regulations. Industry could do more, but it will not. It would be like a ball game with no umpire; I would hate to see the day when you would have 18 umpires. Industry has no way to control the chiseler — *Labor Relations and Personnel Administrator, Chemicals*

*   *

I think that you cannot leave many things such as the proper rights of people (workers, consumers, the public) in the hands of the industry alone. There is too much basic greed generally prevalent in the industry — success is based on profits and profit is too much of an incentive in everything — *General Manager, Heavy Machinery*

*   *

Industry cannot regulate itself; in every industry there are corporations that are real manipulators who take advantage of any opening, and other corporations that need protection from the government — *Manager, Operations, Tires*

The minority simply said that industry can police itself, and that government regulations are not necessary, but many gave more specific responses that: (1) market pressures themselves help industry to police itself, and (2) industry associations can help to regulate industry. Several commented that the government should simply provide regulatory guidelines and not become involved in making detailed industrywide regulations. Although some government regulations might be needed, there should be only a few. The suggestion was made, furthermore, that there should be greater cooperation between government and industry in framing the regulations, a procedure that has been carried out in some agencies for many years.

Industry can be regulated by the customer through competitive selection. Even an industry or corporation could not keep its employees if it were unsafe or unfair to labor. Of course, some workers would have no choice, as in many coal mine areas — *Factory Manager, Division, Heavy Machinery*

*   *

Competitive systems can regulate an industry to a degree. But at the initial stages of development of new practices, there must be some government regulation. Once established, then government can cut back on the regulations — *Manager, Business Practices, Business Equipment*

*   *

I think that they need government guidelines, but not strict government controls. Industry can regulate itself within that type of framework — *Budget Coordinator, Missiles, Aerospace*

*   *

The aluminum industry does a good job of self-regulation. All industries could do as well, but they will not. It depends somewhat on the position of the dominant corporation or some dominant top management in the industry — *Manager, Employee Benefits, Aluminum*

*   *

Industries can regulate themselves in part. The situation needs a lot less regulation than it has. It does not hurt, however, to have someone (e.g., government) looking over your shoulder in a corporate situation, provided they are fair-minded — *Manager, Marketing Division, Auto Industry*

*   *

I think that industry can police itself generally, but there must be some governmental control. Government cannot afford enough qualified inspectors, and therefore the industry must do its own policing — *Production Process Engineer, Auto Industry*

*   *

The steel, copper, etc. industries can regulate themselves without government regulations. But the government must authorize self-regulation. Some government regulations prevent corporations from doing their own regulating — *Assistant Treasurer, Steel*

*   *

We could regulate the auto industry without goverment, including safety regulations. Management would be more responsible if there were no government regulations. The present situation leaves it up to the government to find the violations. Industry could then put out a better and a more competitive car — *General Purchasing Agent, Auto Industry*

*   *

I think industry can regulate itself. The competitive system in the country would be the best from all points of view to keep industry self-regulated. We do not need the government — *Manager, Wholesale Department, Tires*

REGULATORY AGENCIES RECOMMENDED FOR RETENTION

Executives were asked about the types of agencies they would like to see retained for their own industries, for other industries, and for the protection of the general public. No list of agencies was provided, and they were simply asked to name them. It was granted that some agency regulations may be excessive and carried to an extreme, but

TABLE 7.1   Regulatory Agencies Recommended for Retention (62 valid cases)

Agency	Number of Responses	Percentage of Responses	Percentage of Cases
Anti-trust (FTC and Justice)	47	20.8	75.8
OSHA (Occupational Safety and Health Administration)	39	17.2	62.9
CPSC (Consumer Product Safety Commission)	38	16.7	61.3
FDA (Food and Drug Administration)	27	11.9	43.5
NLRB (National Labor Relations Board)	20	8.8	32.3
EEOC (Equal Employment Opportunity Commission)	13	5.7	21.0
SEC (Security and Exchange Commission)	9	4.0	14.5
EPA (Environmental Protection Agency)	5	2.2	8.1
FAA (Federal Aviation Administration)	3	1.3	4.8
Other	26	11.5	41.9
Total	227	100.0	—

that this fact should not influence their own view of the importance of what should be regulated by government. By total responses, they believed that the most important agencies, in order of importance, were: Anti-trust (Federal Trade Commission and Justice), the Occupational Safety and Health Administration (OSHA), the Consumer Product Safety Commission (CPSC), and the Food and Drug Administration (FDA). In terms of the percentage of executives who mentioned a given agency, nearly three-fourths of them mentioned Anti-trust, two-thirds OSHA and CPSC, and about half, FDA. In view of extensive criticisms from the business world, it is surprising that executives would rank OSHA as second in importance, but most of them stated that they had been impressed with the great need for worker safety. In fact, worker and consumer safety generally ranked high in their opinions (see Table 7.1).

The order of agency importance changed slightly when their first choices (62 cases) were considered: the order was Anti-trust (FTC and Justice), CPSC, OSHA, NLRB, FDA, EEOC, SEC, and EPA. In view of the fact that the interviewees were retired businessmen who presumably still have financial interests, it is somewhat surprising that the Securities and Exchange Commission's importance was mentioned by only one out of seven as a first choice, and in one out of twenty of the total responses.

REPORTING CORPORATE VIOLATIONS

Middle management executives were asked: "Do you believe that an employee of a corporation should report to government authorities *serious* violations of the law that have been reported through channels up to the highest corporate authorities but have not been corrected?" Responses were fairly divided, with 53.1 percent saying yes and 46.9 percent no. No significant statistical differences were found in responses in terms of executives' treatment by the corporation or by length of retirement. Respondents who had no college degrees, however, were much less likely (half as much) to believe that a serious violation should be reported to government. Practically no difference was found between responses by those in manufacturing and in marketing. Executives from the chemical and the drug and cosmetic industries were the most likely to believe that serious violations should be reported; those most opposed were in the metals industry.

Respondents were strongly in favor of reporting serious worker safety violations, but when questioned about pricefixing, serious illegal rebates and kickbacks, and illegal payments to foreign officials, they expressed a strong negative view about their being reported to the government (see Table 7.2). In all questions, the respondents were asked to assume that they had incontrovertible evidence that the violations had actually taken place and that nothing had been done about them.

The statistical differences, as measured by chi squares, between reporting serious violations generally and/or serious safety violations, on the one hand, and illegal rebates, kickbacks, and foreign payments, on the other, were highly significant. Pricefixing would also have been highly significant but for the small number in one cell. A sharp distinction was drawn between the reporting of worker safety violations that may cause injuries, and that are therefore serious, and other violations like pricefixing, kickbacks, and foreign payoffs that involved only

TABLE 7.2   Percentage Differences in Reporting Violations to Government

Violation	Yes	No
Serious violations generally	53.1	46.9
Serious unsafe working conditions	69.8	30.2
Pricefixing	23.4	76.6
Illegal rebates and kickbacks	31.7	68.3
Illegal foreign payments	35.5	64.5

monetary losses or payments and thus are not serious in nature (in the opinion of the respondents).

Overall, therefore, the executives generally regarded "serious corporate violations" to be exclusive of pricefixing, illegal rebates and kickbacks, and illegal payments to foreign officials. This implies that no matter how serious they are considered by the law, violations of this type are regarded as something the government is obliged to discover, without assistance from corporate personnel. This is a quite different view from that held in cases of ordinary law violations, where citizens are expected to report them to legal authorities like the police, even though, for various reasons, this is not always done.

Several basic themes were expressed in the reasons for not reporting various types of violations to the government. In order, they were: (1) strong corporate loyalty precludes going to the government ("let the government find out about it"); (2) less government control is needed (though one executive did say: "I think we owe a greater loyalty to our country than to the corporation"); (3) an employee might not have all the pertinent facts about the violation; (4) it would make one's supervisors look bad; and (5) an individual should quit instead of going to the government (one said: "I would report it, but would get the hell out of the corporation"). Some typical comments were:

One must have loyalty to the corporation, once hired— *Manager, Marketing Support, Aerospace*

*   *

We should have as little government as possible —*Plant Manager, Aluminum*

*   *

One must have strong loyalty to corporate superiors, even persons one does not like — *Plant Manager, Aluminum*

*   *

A corporate employee must know all of the facts before going to the government — *General Manager, Marketing, Steel*

*   *

Government should find out about it — *District Sales Manager, Chemicals*

*   *

One should not go to government; one should quit instead — *Production Process Engineer, Auto Industry*

*   *

If you plan to do this (that is, report to government), how many years are you from retirement? — *District Sales Manager, Steel*

*   *

I do not have that much regard for government controls. What is an individual sent out by government going to do about a given situation? — *Manager, Business Practices, Business Equipment*

*   *

Violations should be handled through the corporation and personnel should follow corporate loyalty — *Chief Engineer, Diesel Design, Auto Industry*

*   *

One should quit or stay on and keep his mouth shut. In a sense it is corporate loyalty — *Assistant Treasurer, Steel*

*   *

I should feel disloyal to the corporation except in the case of unsafe working conditions — *Manager, Automotive Marketing, Auto Industry*

*   *

On my way out of the corporation I would report the violation — *Sales Manager, Parts Division, Business Machines*

*   *

You have to have faith in the corporation and top management and therefore not report violations to the government — *National Accounts Manager, Health Care*

*   *

By reporting it in corporate channels I would have done my job — *Advanced Design Engineer, Auto Industry*

*   *

He should get the hell out of there. So long as he is accepting a paycheck he owes a loyalty to the corporation — *Manager, Public Relations, Building Materials*

*   *

If an employee reports to the government, others might do so, and this might encourage unjustified reports of violations — *Labor Relations and Personnel Administrator, Chemicals*

*   *

It is not an employee's responsibility to report corporate violations to any outside source, including government. This applies to middle management as well. This is corporate loyalty — *Operations Manager, Tires*

Executives who believed that violations should be reported to the government took the position that (1) they were law violations; (2) an executive has a responsibility to be honest; and (3) any deliberate violation, and particularly those related to worker or public safety, should be reported.

Unsafe Working Conditions

Seven out of ten executives took strong positions in favor of reporting safety violations to the government. The difference between reporting *serious* worker safety violations and *serious* violations generally was highly significant statistically. As already indicated in the strong support shown for the OSHA, the executives believed that the protection of worker safety was one of the most important responsibilities of any corporation. Workers should not be injured on the job, and if they are not protected, they should turn to the government. As might be expected, because of the nature of their work, those in manufacturing were much more in favor (81.0 percent) of reporting serious worker safety violations than were those in marketing (54.2 percent). Typical comments in favor of and against reporting serious safety violations were:

An employee has to protect his fellow workers from serious unsafe working conditions — *Labor Relations and Personnel Administration, Chemicals*

*   *

This strikes at a man's fundamental integrity if he does not report a serious corporate safety violation — *Assistant to Vice-President of Manufacturing, in Charge of Paint Production, Chemicals*

*   *

Even if he were going to be fired, providing he felt strong enough about the situation — *Design Engineer, Auto Industry*

*   *

Because they are serious and, therefore, safety violations they should be reported to the government — *Operations Manager, Food Processing*

*   *

If serious violations occurred and top management did nothing it has to be reported, but I would get the hell out of that corporation — *Western Divisional Manager, Marketing, Appliances*

*   *

Otherwise, somebody could be hurt, and I do not want to see that — *Supervisor, Technical Services, Petro-Chemical Department, Oil*

*   *

Definitely. Unsafe working conditions constitute a hazard to the employees — *General Purchasing Agent, Engineering Staff Division, Auto Industry*

*   *

Safety is something else and should be reported to the government — *Manager, Automotive Marketing, Auto Industry*

*   *

No man should be killed or seriously hurt on the job — *Senior Processing Engineer, Electrical*

*   *

Safety is the corporation's business and it is not necessary to go to the government — *Division Sales Manager, Oil*

*   *

What is a serious safety violation could be a matter of opinion — *Manager, Project Planning, Building Materials*

*   *

Safety violations should be reported only to management. The employee has no alternatives but to quit or to live with the situation — *National Accounts Manager, Health Supplies*

*   *

They should put up with it or quit. You cannot run to the government for everything — *General Manager, Retail and Wholesale Marketing, Steel*

*   *

I would find another way such as a local broadcaster, rather than go to the government — *Factory Manager, Heavy Machinery*

Pricefixing

In the case of pricefixing, the question was stated in this manner: "Say that you, as middle management, have incontrovertible evidence that prices have been fixed by top management in collusion with your competitors. Someone in the front office has slipped you a copy of a confidential and secret pricing agreement between your top management and those of competitors. Should you report it to government authorities?" Three out of four respondents said that they would not report pricefixing, in spite of the fact that the law regards it as a serious offense with a penalty that can be three years imprisonment and a $1 million corporate fine. Practically no difference was expressed by manufacturing (76.2 percent) and marketing executives (80.0 percent), both largely having the opinion that pricefixing should not be reported. The reporting of pricefixing was supported most strongly by those in the drug and cosmetics industry, and least strongly in metals and aerospace. This strong opposition to reporting pricefixing violations appears to be in contradiction to the view that the control of anti-trust violations is the most important function of all agencies regulating corporate behavior.

The specific reasons given for not reporting pricefixing were that (1) this is a problem of top management and not one of concern to middle management; (2) pricefixing is particularly difficult to prove and one cannot always be certain of the facts; (3) pricefixing is not a serious offense anyway; and (4) in some businesses, pricefixing is necessary to bring some order into the competition.

I am not so disturbed about pricefixing — *Contract Estimator, Aerospace*

*   *

This is a difficult law. It is easy for corporations to exchange information about competitive prices — *District Sales Manager, Steel*

*   *

It is not my responsibility since it is a problem of top management. Anyway, pricefixing is not a clear cut violation — *Vice President, Manufacturing Division, Paper*

*   *

Pricefixing involves money and not people's safety or the national interest — *Director, Business Development, Toiletries*

*   *

It is difficult to be aware of the facts in pricefixing. It would be disloyal to the corporation to report it to government — *General Purchasing Agent, Auto Industry*

*   *

Pricefixing is not that serious on a long-term basis — *Supervisor, Technical Services, Oil*

*   *

It is none of my business. As a plant manager, pricefixing did not affect me personally as did worker safety — *Manager, Manufacturing Facility Planning, Farm Equipment*

*   *

Pricefixing is none of middle management's damn business. If there is a general in charge you do not blow the whistle on him — *Manager, International Division, Steel*

*   *

He should not be a "stool pigeon." After all, top management already knows about it because it has done it — *Marketing Manager, European Division, Foods*

*   *

I am not running the corporation. I am not the CEO. I am in middle management and pricefixing is not my business — *Advanced Design Engineer, Auto Industry*

*   *

Am I God that I should go to the government on a top management pricefixing agreement and sacrifice myself? — *Plant Manager, Auto Industry*

*   *

If top management does not want to do anything about it, why should I? — *Director, Public Relations, Foods*

*   *

Not middle management's problem. In our industry, pricefixing has a long history — *Manager, Public Relations, Building Materials*

*   *

I was not hired to protect prices for consumers — *Manager, Management Engineering, Aerospace*

*   *

You can leave your job and then you can make a formal complaint
to government — *Operations Management, Tires*

*   *

I do not consider it to be the job of middle management to act as a
policeman in pricefixing — *Manager, International Marketing Division, Chemicals*

Illegal Rebates and Kickbacks

Two out of three executives were not in favor of reporting illegal
rebates and kickbacks to the government. As might be expected, due
to the closer connection of these offenses to marketing, executives
working in these areas were much more opposed (79.2 percent) than
were those in manufacturing (61.9 percent). Many had similar views
about pricefixing. It is, above all, not a concern of middle management,
but must be left to top management. Second, such practices are
customary in many industries, and third, the government should be
able to find out about these violations without help from corporate
personnel.

I would not get involved in reporting illegal rebates or kickbacks
— *Director, Business Development, Farm Equipment*

*   *

It is not the government's business. I usually got enough gifts
from suppliers to fill the bedroom. I gave them all away — *General
Purchasing Agent, Auto Industry*

*   *

Rebates and kickbacks are too prevalent in many industries; it
would not be worth it to get fired — *District Manager, Sales
Division, Metals*

*   *

It is not my business as middle management to get involved.
Illegal rebates and kickbacks are a fairly common corporate practice in my industry — *Production Manager, Paper*

*   *

I would not report it unless it involved a government contract — *Factory Manager, Division, Heavy Equipment*

     *   *

We might lose business if we did not give illegal rebates and kickbacks — *Division Manager, Machinery*

     *   *

Because it is a common business practice I would not report it to government — *Materials Manager, Light Industry*

Illegal Payments to Foreign Officials

Two out of three executives held the view that illegal payments to foreign officials should not be reported. Almost identical opposition was expressed by manufacturing and marketing executives. They gave several reasons for not reporting them: (1) illegal foreign payments are the concern of top management, not theirs; (2) it is necessary to bribe officials in order to compete for contracts in foreign countries; and (3) it would be disloyal to the corporation should they go to the government.

It is necessary to make payments abroad to beat out foreign competition — *General Manager, Marketing, Steel*

     *   *

I would not report it because of my loyalty to the corporation — *Director, Business Development, Farm Equipment*

     *   *

It is none of my business what the corporation does in overseas bribery — *General Purchasing Agent, Auto Industry*

     *   *

It is not my responsibility as middle management. If I were a vice president I would do it — *Manager of Operations, Foods*

In spite of the frequent claims of spokesmen for corporate business that there is almost complete unanimity in the corporate world about the need to pay foreign bribes, it is significant that as high as one out of three interviewees felt: (1) that such bribes should be reported to the government since they are not legal; (2) that it is unethical to bribe foreign officials, and (3) that it presents an unfavorable image of the United States abroad. In fact, two executives who had worked abroad said that the bribery of foreign officials is definitely illegal, that it should be reported (a tire manufacturing executive), and that it is dangerous as a corporate practice to bribe foreign officials (chemical industry executive). Other typical comments included the following:

> So much scandal has been created by Lockheed and others in illegal foreign payments that it has hurt all of us. We could probably have gotten the foreign business for an American concern anyway — *Executive Vice President, Foods*

> *   *

> I have worked all over the world, and I was never asked to give a corporate bribe. Actually many such bribes are offered by corporations to get business — *Manager, International Marketing Division, Chemicals*

> *   *

> It is against the principles of all decency to bribe foreign officials — *Supervisor, Technical Services, Oil*

> *   *

> If you give a bribe to a foreign official they should have the same opportunity to bribe American officials — *Division Sales Manager, Oil*

> *   *

> I think that I am so bitter about our difficult overseas situation that I believe that foreign bribes would make it even worse — *Manager, Wholesale Department, Tires*

> *   *

> Damned right I would report it. I never did like giving bribes to foreign officials. I do not see why we need to do this to do business abroad — *Materials Manager, Light Industry*

SHOULD EMPLOYEES WHO REPORT VIOLATIONS BE PROTECTED BY GOVERNMENT?

The question was asked: If an employee, including management personnel, did report a serious violation of regulations to the government — "blowing the whistle" — should that person be protected by law from dismissal? This issue involves the broader question of corporate employees' freedom of speech, consisting in part of "(1) the right to refuse immoral orders from superiors and (2) the right to complain about potentially dangerous products or potentially dangerous practices" (Donaldson, 1982: 145). In spite of the generally negative view toward reporting many types of violations to the government, three out of four (74.6 percent) respondents felt that corporate employees should be protected from dismissal. A considerably larger proportion of those in marketing (79.2 percent) than in manufacturing (66.7 percent) felt this way. Those most likely to support employee protection were aerospace executives; those least in favor of it were metal industry executives.

The chief reasons for wanting employee protection were: (1) one should not be penalized for doing what one believes to be right, and (2) one should be able to go to the government without fear of dismissal. Many respondents hastened to add, however, that such a report must stem from a serious violation and a genuine desire to have the violation corrected, and should not be because of a grudge against the corporation. In the long run, however, to make such a report to the government would generally be harmful to the individual employee. One out of four of the total sample of respondents was of the opinion that any employees who reported violations to the government would subsequently be put in an uncomfortable position regarding salaries and promotions, and that they might even be harassed. So difficult might it become for them that their positions might be endangered, and they should probably not continue to work for the corporation.

He should be protected. I feel strongly about protecting those government employees who have done so — *Manager, Business Practices, Business Equipment*

*   *

He is doing it for society's benefit. This takes precedence over corporate loyalty — *Manager, Management Engineering, Aerospace*

*   *

He should be protected like any other person who reports a law violation to the police — *Manager, Western Division Marketing, Foods*

*   *

His opportunities within the corporation, however, would be limited afterwards — *Director, Research Administration, Chemicals*

*   *

It is highly unsatisfactory to have one's job protected in that way. He should go somewhere else — *Supervisor, Technical Services, Oil*

*   *

Even if I did report violations to the government I would not last long; they would find a way to get rid of me — *District Manager, Sales Division, Metals*

*   *

What will happen afterwards to him in the corporation is something else — *Production Director, Tires*

*   *

His job would be difficult after that. He might even have difficulties in finding a job in another corporation — *Regional Marketing Manager, Oil*

*   *

By all means he should be protected by government, but no law could protect him from the rage of the corporation — *Director, Corporate Taxes, Chemicals*

*   *

But life in the corporation afterwards would be most miserable — you might be counting paper clips — *Materials Manager, Light Industry*

*   *

If not protected, forces in the corporation would come down on him and he probably would be fired — *Assistant to Vice President, Manufacturing, Paints*

Those who felt that an employee should not be protected based their reasoning chiefly on the assumptions that (1) such protection would constitute disloyalty to the corporation, and (2) the facts about the violation would have to be conclusive, which would not in general be the case. Moreover, several felt that rather than seeking such protection, the employee should quit.

Employee protection would open up a big can of worms. Lawyers, for example, could even file suits to help protect the employee — *Plant Manager, Aluminum*

*   *

Any employee should have the right, but he is going to get the works. He would be a fool — *Manager, Employee Benefits, Aluminum*

*   *

How could he continue to work in such a situation? — *Executive Vice President, Foods*

*   *

How practical is it? He would not go very far in the corporation after being kept in the job by law — *Director, Engineering, Chemicals*

*   *

Why should he want to go back to the corporation? I am in general against government interference with industry — *Plant Manager, Auto Industry*

*   *

He should not be protected from dismissal because reporting to the government reflects on his corporate loyalty — *Operations Manager, Tires*

*   *

At no time could I see a corporate employee going to government about violations — *Operations Manager, Tires*

*   *

He would have a miserable existence in the corporation. He should be protected in government, however, for government employees are working for the public — *Manager, Public Relations, Building Materials*

*   *

I am strongly against them taking corporate rights to dismiss an employee away from them — *General Manager, Heavy Machinery*

*   *

He would have chosen to live by personal ethical standards as opposed to corporate standards. He should find another corporation more compatible with his own values — *Manager, Western Division Marketing, Oil*

*   *

Probably will not get anywhere in the corporation afterwards, so why protect him? — *Manager, Recording Development, Records*

In conclusion, some of the views of these executives regarding the role of government were not what one might have expected from products of the corporate social system. In other respects, they were exactly what one might anticipate. The presence of government regulation, according to the majority of the interviewees, did not contribute substantially to a negative attitude conducive to violations. Moreover, nearly three out of four thought that government regulation is needed and that industry cannot really police itself. They expressed particularly strong views about the necessity for anti-trust laws and regulations to protect worker safety and health.

On the other hand, opinions were mixed about reporting serious violations to the government where nothing had been done about them at the highest corporate levels. Slightly over half of the interviewees said that they would tend to report serious violations in general, and three out of four would report serious worker safety violations. For a number of reasons, however, they said that they would not routinely report pricefixing, illegal rebates or kickbacks, nor illegal foreign payments. Three out of four would like to have the government protect any employee who reported a serious corporate violation, although most of them felt that such an employee's corporate future would be questionable.

8

INTERPRETATION

The organizational structure of any large corporation rests funda-
mentally on the relationships between many persons, including the
board of directors, top management, middle management, supervisory personnel, and workers. In this hierarchical social structure, as
has been pointed out, middle management plays a crucial role, as it is
they who are responsible for carrying out top management's
directives. Their accomplishments in this role affect the success of
procurement, manufacturing, marketing, and other areas of the
corporate structure. Moreover, middle management occupies a focal
point in organizational interrelations between senior management and
the supervisory staff. Although the views of top management about
corporate ethics and illegal behavior have been the subject of scientific
study (Silk and Vogel, 1976), in no previous study has an attempt been
made to learn the views of middle management. Through lengthy
interviews, this study has looked at the organizational relationships of
a large corporation as seen by a sample of retired Fortune 500 middle
management executives. Unfortunately, it was not possible to obtain a
truly representative sample of Fortune 500 middle management;
however, the sample was so varied by type of industry, size of
corporation, type of position in the corporation, age, and education
that it resulted in a somewhat stratified sample. Inasmuch as their
views had been developed through long experience, they should be
regarded as important. What they have to say about corporate ethics
and illegal behavior should increase our understanding of the processes
within a corporation that account for this behavior.

One problem remains unanswered: To what extent do these views coincide with the existing literature in the diverse areas presented, and what further implications might be drawn from their interview statements? Here an analysis is made, first, of the internal and external factors that affect corporate behavior, and then of the inferences of their views for the social control of unethical and illegal corporate behavior.

INTERNAL FACTORS

The middle management executives emphasized internal factors within their corporations as the chief causative factors for unethical and illegal behavior, with the two most important being the role of top management and the various corporate pressures placed on middle management. As previously indicated, business ethics were defined as fairness and honesty to the public, the consumer, competitors, and the government. The line distinguishing ethics and law violations is often not clear, and many corporate practices formerly considered to be simply unethical have now become illegal and thus subject to punishment. As one middle management executive put it: "Law violations are about the same as ethics except in the former you go to jail."

The Role of Top Management

From an organizational point of view, as has been indicated before, unethical practices and law violations within a corporation can sometimes be attributed to the *internal* structure of a corporation rather than to such *external* factors as the unfair practices of competitors, or to a corporation's difficult financial position in the market. Moreover, the complex structural relationships within large corporations often make it difficult, in cases of unethical or illegal behavior, to disentangle delegated authority, managerial discretion, and the ultimate responsibility of top management. Throughout the interviews, the general theme expressed by most middle management executives was that top management, and in particular the chief executive officer (CEO), sets the corporate ethical tone. These views were not found to be due to antagonisms or to jealousy of top management as such; the respondents simply felt that top management completely dominated the overall ethical tone of their corporations. Over half of the interviewees went even further, believing top management to be directly responsibile for the violation of government regulations. In fact, top management's influence takes precedence, in their views, over the possibility of a preexisting ethical (or non-ethical) general corporate cultural pattern. One executive described the prime role of top management succinctly when he said:

> Ethics comes and goes in a corporation according to who is in top management. I worked under four corporation presidents, and each differed — first was honest, next was a "wheeler-dealer," the third was somewhat better, and the last one was bad. According to their ethical views, pressures were put on middle management all the way down.

Middle management's views about this decisive role of top management in setting the ethical standards of a corporation are in line with most of the literature in the field. One recent study of employee theft in large corporations, for example, found that when the integrity, fairness, and ethical standards of a corporation itself and of its top management were questioned by the workers, property and production deviance were also more likely to be found (Clark and Hollinger, 1982). After he had surveyed various data, Gross (1978: 71) concluded that "persons who will engage in crime on behalf of the organization will most likely be the officers of the organization, its top people." In elaborating this conclusion, he states:

> In sum, then, the men at the top of organizations will tend to be ambitious, shrewd and possessed of a nondemanding moral code. Their ambition will not be merely personal, for they will have discovered that their own goals are best pursued through assisting the organization to attain its goals. While this is less true, or even untrue at the bottom of the organization, those at the top share directly in the benefits of organizational goal achievement, such as seeing their stock values go up, deferred compensation, and fringe benefits [Gross, 1978: 71].

A recent comprehensive study of corporations concluded: "That top managers generally control large corporations is an established truth, which serves as a premise — not something to be proved — in most serious analyses in the field of industrial organization and policy" (Herman, 1981: 14).[1] Neither the board of directors nor the stockholders are actually in charge of running a corporation, although large holders like financial institutions and large family holdings may have some general influence on policy. The basis of top management control, or "managerism," lies in its strategic position and its decision making. Role and status in corporate organizations, such as being a CEO, president, or chairman of the board, enable their possessors to participate in key decisions not only about finances, but also about the ethical direction of a corporation in relation to workers, consumers, competitors, and the government.

> Strategic position is the crucial underpinning of management control of the large corporation. It rests on daily and direct (top) management command over personnel and resources, knowledge, the importance of managerial and organizational skills, and the structural and social relationships that develop on the basis of proximate command. The power lacunae left by the diffusion of ownership is [sic] gradually occupied by those who exercise power on a daily basis and who are thereby well positioned to consolidate it more firmly over time. Management's control is facilitated by its domination of the board selection processes and the resultant capacity of top officials to mold boards into friendly and compliant bodies [Herman, 1981: 52].

Top corporate managers possess great autonomy and, therefore, considerable power in making decisions regarding production, investments, pricing, and marketing. The internal corporate master of the executive is the "bottom line"; often it is corporate profits, not morality, that provide the ultimate test of the effectiveness of top management. "If external forces drive the executive to meet the challenge of innovative competition, the internal forces push the executive towards learning how to use power to achieve the ends set by the external environment" (Madden, 1977: 71). Their very rank generates identity, power, and the many "perks" that go with it (De Mare, 1976). Those in control of corporations "pay themselves generously, and, under the impetus of high personal tax rates, have developed elaborate systems of compensation by deferred money payments, stock options and bonuses, and expense account perquisites of large scope and ingenuity" (Herman, 1981: 248). A psychiatrist who specializes in dealing with chief executive officers under stress describes their corporate roles, and in so doing indicates some of their personal problems:

> The boss needs no praise. He's like a god. He's omnipotent. So, looking upward, people always overestimate the power of their boss. Downward, the boss underestimates his subordinates. People attribute all sorts of power to the chief executive. And many chief executives want to buy into that belief. And that's a very serious situation. They can't stand to lose face, to admit any weakness [Kleinfield, 1982].

Middle management executives appear to have correctly minimized the role of the board of directors in decision making by their corporations; they hardly ever mentioned their boards of directors. As one writer has stated: "One immediate problem confronting any attempt to improve corporate morality by shifting power among board members is that corporate boards of directors frequently exercise only minimal control over their respective companies" (Donaldson, 1982: 189). Legally, the power to control corporate officers rests with the board of directors and, through them, the stockholders. Although the board of directors "controls" the corporation in a legal sense, in actuality almost all major corporate decisions are "shared in or finally decided upon by a small group of high-level leaders of the organization" (Herman, 1981: 23). Even on the board, top inside managers generally dominate the decision-making process, as well as the selection of new board members. Outsiders on the board, however, may actively exercise their legal powers under circumstances such as the serious nonperformance, or malfeasance, of top management. Thus, the stability of control by top management can be undermined by the board of directors under traumatic conditions.

> Revelations of illegal acts, serious conflicts of interest brought to light, major antitrust actions — reduce the prestige of management, threaten it with legal action and negative publicity, and adversely affect organizational unity and morale. They provide the vehicles through which opponents of the management may organize attacks against it. The Dorsey management of Gulf Oil was ousted following a corporate trauma that unleashed latent

antimanagement forces that were not only disturbed by the adverse publicity [about violations] but were also disenchanted by Gulf's economic performance over the prior several years [Herman, 1981: 50-51].

Types of Top Executives

In the opinion of many middle management executives, top management's particular character and personality often influence the internal structure of the corporation. Some "financially oriented" executives, for example, are interested primarily in securing financial prestige and quick profits for the corporation, as well as increased compensation for themselves. These top executives are likely to engage to a greater extent in unethical practices than are the more "technical and professional types" who have been trained in such specialized areas as engineering. As one executive said: "Our CEO was a technical man, an engineer, and not a financially oriented person interested in the fast buck." Illustrating this distinction is a study of prescription violations (Quinney, 1963/1967) in which it was found that the professional retail type of pharmacist was far less likely to violate the law than the business-oriented type.

A similar distinction, although different in terminology, has been made between "fiduciary" top managers and "entrepreneurial" managers (Evan, 1976: 90). Fiduciary managers have an ethical commitment of service to beneficiaries; they do not make self-serving decisions, and they try to promote the interests of the organization as a corporate entity. On the other hand, the entrepreneurial manager governs the corporate body entirely on behalf of the owners, and his behavior is directed exclusively toward the corporation's profit maximization. One interviewee contrasted these types:

> My personal feeling is that those corporations that are unethical are managed by persons (CEOs) who are highly competitive, wanting to improve the corporation's profit margins and thinking that they will not get caught. Such CEOs are trying to improve their personal positions and that of their corporation. The only way to do it is often unethical.

Still another distinction was drawn between the ethics of top management persons who tend to be mobile, moving from one corporation to another, and being recruited into a corporation from the outside. These executives are more likely to be aggressive, interested in their own rapid corporate achievements and consequent publicity in financial journals; they have limited concern for the corporation's long-term reputation. One interviewee described this type of executive:

> The upper management structure, particularly the CEO, leads to unethical practices. They are the "Go-Go" type of managers. Such a CEO does not intend to stay for more than two years, and he cares little about the corporation's reputation. Like sharks, they gobble up other corporations. Such CEOs end up with lots of executive perks and their names are favorably mentioned as go-getters in *The Wall Street Journal* and in *Fortune*.

In contrast to these executives are those top executives who have come up from the ranks as workers, supervisors, or middle managers, particularly in production; they have had a long-term indoctrination into the corporate history, product quality, and pride in the corporation. They tend to occupy top management positions for lengthy periods of time, and they are less likely to tarnish the corporate name by permitting the corporation to engage in unethical or illegal behavior. The literature somewhat supports this view. Herman (1981: 51) states that the "length of time of top inside management also affects stability of control."

Studied from a somewhat different perspective, the prior corporate situation in top management is important. If the founder or subsequent strong executives had established a long history of expected ethical practices, two results can be anticipated. New top executives will be recruited to fit this pattern, or else top executives will tend to go along with the established corporate practices of doing business, as Vaughan (1982: 1389) has pointed out: "It is common knowledge that organizations selectively recruit new members who in many ways match those already there. . . . Because business firms depend on their members' skills to attain goals, they must ensure that members' motivations and values are consistent with the organization's needs." This view has been confirmed in a study of the fifteen best-run large U.S. corporations (Peters and Waterman, 1982). Most of these corporations bear the imprint of a few titanic figures who were often in command for decades and who created, and left, an atmosphere of corporate achievement and excellence that was conveyed to employees.[2]

Others have not made the distinction in the types of top managers that was made here by the middle management interviewees, as well as by some other writers. Instead, they have pointed with a broad brush to the personal characteristics of all those who have made it to the top of large-scale organizations (see Gross, 1978: 67-72). Gross believes that all are characterized by excessive ambition and competitiveness. Others have said it this way: "The meek shall not inherit top management" (Lewis and Stewart, 1961). Other prevailing characteristics include shrewdness and moral flexibility, the latter being the ability "to change his moral beliefs with little distress so that they match whatever is called for by the organization" (Gross, 1978: 69). One study reported that when conflict arises between personal and organizational values, those top managers who find the organization distasteful to their own values tend to leave the organization (Dill et al., 1962). When Gross shifts to the types of top managers who would be *more likely* to be involved in corporate crime, however, he comes close to what the middle management executives called the "financial type" of top management:

> Persons who actually act for the organization in the commission of such crimes will, by selective processes associated with upward mobility in organizations, be persons likely to he highly committed to the organization and be, for various reasons, willing and able to carry out crime, should it seem to be required in order to enable the organization to attain its goals, to prosper, or, minimally, to survive [Gross, 1978: 72].

Lines of Communication

One gets the general impression from middle management interviewees that the lines of communication within their corporations were quite open and that top management would know about violations either before they occurred or shortly thereafter. Empirical data from other research on corporate crime support these conclusions. The senior management of most corporations, for example, knew about the pricefixing in the well-known folding carton case of 1976 (Clinard and Yeager, 1980: 279). One corporate executive said: "The fact that meetings were held and price information was exchanged was well known to the senior management of the (23) corporations involved." Of those corporate executives originally involved in the folding carton conspiracy, nineteen had middle management level responsibility, and ten were from top management. In a study of 46 corporations involved in questionable domestic or foreign commercial payments or kickbacks, and which were reported to the SEC, top management knew about them in all but eight corporations; in 24 cases, nearly all top management knew about them (Clinard and Yeager, 1980: 279-280). The violations were known individually to three board chairmen, five chief executive officers, six presidents, five executive presidents, and eleven vice presidents. In five corporations they were known to the combined board chairmen and chief executive officer, and in two corporations where the offices of president and CEO were combined.

As opposed to the middle management view, the claim is often made by others that within a corporation, the delegation of authority and reliance on general directives and unwritten orders tend to isolate top management from the legal consequences of their policy decisions. Often top management does not know what is actually being done by middle management. Top management may "arrange patterns of reporting so they cannot find out (or, at least, if they do find out, they find out in such a way that it can never by proved)" (Stone, 1975: 53). Thus executives at the top levels can absolve themselves of responsibility by claiming that illegal means of obtaining corporate goals were used without their knowledge. Moreover, at both top and middle management levels there may be tacit agreements to perpetuate the lack of exchange of full information, since the key to successful corporate law violation may lie in the fact that top management does not ask about what is going on, and middle management does not tell them. One survey reported that top managers may not be aware that some subordinates commit unethical acts out of loyalty to the firm or to their superiors (Carroll, 1975). Two writers have bluntly stated their views of the frequent lack of communication within the corporate hierarchy:

> The presidents of some of the largest firms in the world point with pride in their speeches about what they are doing to clean up the environment. What they don't know is that some of their plant superintendents are still dumping poison into the rivers or sending them out the stacks . . . at night [Barnet and Miller, 1974: 345].

One study found that the percentage of middle management executives reporting that their inability to be honest in providing important information to top management about unethical behavior or violations of the law had almost doubled since the 1950s (Baumhart, 1961; Brenner and Molander, 1977). It is claimed that within more recent years, this lack of communication seems to have become a primary source of conflict between corporations' interests and the personal ethics of middle management (Brenner and Molander, 1977). If this is true (and the interviewees in our middle management sample strongly disagreed), the resulting lack of knowledge about certain practices of middle management may provide some legal protection when government prosecutors try to idenfity precisely who is liable within the corporate hierarchy.

Pressures on Middle Management

Middle management executives tended to feel that corporate pressures at their level were extensive and serious. Undue pressures from top management, they maintained, may result in unethical or illegal behavior. Few of the interviewees reported any personal involvement; however, these pressures greatly affect the lives of a large proportion of middle management executives, the greatest being to show profits and to keep cost in line. Time pressures and production and sales quotas were also significant.

Middle management's feelings about the undue pressures exerted on them have been supported by a number of research studies. One study of 186 middle and senior managers of a multinational corporation found that middle managers tended to experience high pressure levels on many work issues. In fact, pressures were found to be the greatest at middle management levels (Marshall and Cooper, 1979). The most common sources of job-related pressures were (1) time pressures, (2) the lack of autonomy in decision making, (3) difficulties in managing people, and (4) job responsibilities. On the other hand, senior management's pressures were of a diffierent type, and job satisfaction was greater. Pressures on them tended to be due to longer working hours, the burden of making decisions and managing people and, to a lesser extent, some lack of autonomy. A similar conclusion was reached in another study, where role conflict and ambiguity were found to be greater at middle management than at either senior or junior management levels (Kahn et al., 1964). In fact, it has been concluded, from national surveys of the views of middle management by the

Opinion Research Corporation over the past 25 years, that middle management job satisfaction, work environment satisfaction, and communication effectiveness have all declined (Cooper et al., 1980). By 1979, these surveys found, middle management felt that top management was both controlling them excessively and increasingly ignoring them. They believed that they were not respected as much as they had been in previous years, that their corporations were becoming increasingly unwilling to listen to them, and that both their job security and advancement opportunities had declined. A survey of more than 500 middle management executives in thirteen large corporations found that only 60 percent felt that their corporation had delivered on its goal of making them feel valued or have a sense of belonging (Cox, 1982: 177).[3]

In a 1970 survey of nearly 3000 executives conducted by the American Management Association, nearly half of the 536 middle managers stated that their jobs were not satisfying to them (DeMaria et al., 1972). They also believed that their companies failed to provide them with sufficient opportunities to realize their own aspirations. They claimed that they were not given a "real" role in corporate decision making, since their ideas were frequently ignored by top management. Although they had a great deal of responsibility in their positions, they had little opportunity to exert much influence.

A later study found that middle management executives were subject to the severe pressures of (1) having little real authority at the levels of their responsibility; (2) being "boxed in," in terms of career inflexibility, restricted job mobility, and career advancement; (3) facing the possibility of forced retirement, which might involve their obsolescence for the corporation in terms of technological, interpersonal, cultural (corporate), political, or economic aspirations; and (4) having to accept "pay compression" as a result of hiring new recruits at higher salaries (Kay, 1974). The lack of real delegation of authority to them by top management concerned authority that was withheld explicitly, uncertain authority, or contingent authority. A 1982 survey of middle managers by the Opinion Research Center found that 69 percent felt that their authority was being eroded, and almost two-thirds cited stress and increased pace as major problems (Cooper et al., 1980).

These studies of pressures looked into the effects on middle managers, subordinates, and the corporation in general. They did not examine, as was done in this study, the possibility that pressures might lead to either unethical or illegal conduct in an effort to achieve corporate goals. A leading analyst of unethical corporate behavior has argued that business executives such as middle managers are, on the whole, intrinsically ethical; they do not change until they have become immersed in the "formlessness" and pressures of a corporation. Even then, they engage in unethical practices for the corporation only after having shed their own individuality (Stone, 1975). After examining contemporary corporations, Herman (1981) concluded that top managers respond to pressures within the organization in making their own decisions. In this process, middle managers have "to limit the range of their direction and press them toward a profit orientation at least as unequivocal as that of owner/managers" (Herman, 1981: 247). As one executive put it:

> You get the pressure so strong from top management that you will make judgmental efforts to make things come out right even if you use unethical practices such as lying about production or marketing progress. Pressures can result in cutting corners, e.g., on quality; a corporation has got to be a going concern.

The ethical effects of pressures put on middle management by their corporations have been confirmed in the only other such study that has been made (Carroll, 1975). In this study top, middle, and lower management executives (none retired) were chosen from *Standard and Poor's Executive Register,* all of whom had been mailed a questionnaire. In this rather brief study, it was found that 65 percent of the middle managers who responded to the questionnaire felt themselves to be under pressure to compromise their own personal standards in order to achieve the goals of their corporations. They also felt that, due to pressures from the top to achieve certain results, middle management compromises occur. In contrast to top management, the majority of middle management personnel felt, moreover, that "the illegal business contributions of the last year or so (Nixon campaign) are realistic examples of ethics of business today." As C. F. Luce, Chairman of Consolidated Edison, has stated: "The top manager has a duty not to push so hard that middle managers are pushed to unethical compromises" (Business Week, 1975). *The Wall Street Journal* (November 8, 1979) has also pointed out that pressures do produce ethical problems.

Middle managers, experts say, are the most likely members of the corporate hierarchy to confront the ethical dilemmas that can arise when the dictum goes out to meet company objectives. Unlike top executives, these managers often have little say in how such goals are set; yet unlike production line workers, whose unions protect them from retribution for occasional shortcomings, a middle manager's future rides almost solely on his ability to serve up whatever the boss demands.

The position taken by middle management executives is also supported by considerable case study material. For example, even though the top General Electric managers involved in the well-publicized heavy electrical product pricefixing conspiracy of the 1960s did not precisely order their middle managers to fix prices, they did put great pressures on them to show higher profits. In order to comply with top management's demands, these middle managers worked out pricefixing agreements with their counterparts at Westinghouse and other electrical manufacturing corporations (Woodmansee, 1975: 50; Geis, 1967; Herling, 1962).

An almost classic case of how middle managers cut corners to achieve high corporate goals is that of the H. J. Heinz Corporation. In 1979 this giant food corporation reported that a profit-juggling scheme, going on within corporate units since 1972, had resulted in increased "profits" estimated at $8.5 million. Due to the deferral and retrieval of income, a practice used by operating managers to help meet company-set profit goals, the corporate per-share earnings in various quarterly periods were understated and overstated (The Wall Street Journal, November 8, 1979). The five-year average earnings should have been 13.5 percent instead of 15.4 percent.

To hear some middle managers there tell it, the "pressure-cooker" atmosphere at Pittsburgh's H. J. Heinz Co. was not confined to the concern's steamy food-processing plants. "When we didn't meet our growth targets the top brass really came down on us," recalls a former marketing official at the company's huge Heinz U.S.A. division. "And everybody knew that if you missed the targets enough, you were out on your ear." In this environment, some harried managers apparently resorted to deceptive bookkeeping when they couldn't otherwise meet profit goals set by the company's top executives. Invoices were misdated and payments to suppliers were made in advance — sometimes to be returned later in cash — all with the aim, insiders say, of showing the sort of smooth profit growth that would please top management and impress securities analysts [The Wall Street Journal, November 8, 1979].

Subsequently, the Heinz Audit Committee Report to the SEC, in 1980, found that even though senior management did not participate in the profit-juggling practices, they "apparently didn't consider the effect on individuals in the affiliates of the pressure to which they were subjected" (The Wall Street Journal, May 9, 1980). In fact, as this same article commented: "The resulting report provides a rare glimpse of the internal operations of a large company, in Heinz's case a decentralized concern whose operating units are allowed to use their own methods as long as they achieved goals set by top management."

EXTERNAL FACTORS

Middle management executives generally expressed the feeling that the source of unethical and illegal behavior lay primarily within the corporation itself, not in external factors. In general, they did not consider as important such external factors as the poor corporate financial situation and unfair competitive practices.

Poor Financial Situation

Only two of the executives interviewed considered a corporation's poor financial situation, such as a decline in profits or their share of the market, as a primary explanation of unethical and illegal behavior; few others even mentioned it. This view was different in context from, though not in contradiction to, the position advanced by many executives that the chief pressure exerted on corporate middle management was to show profits and to keep costs in line.

This opinion has been supported, on the whole, by a major study of the role of their financial situation in the illegal behavior of Fortune 500 corporations (Clinard et al., 1979; Clinard and Yeager, 1980). The study failed to find a substantial relationship between the two; instead, it found that one must look largely to internal factors for an explanation of corporate violations. The study concluded:

> The violating firms are on average larger, less financially successful, experience relatively poorer growth rates and are more diversified. However, the relationships were only of moderate strength at best. When combined in statistical models to maximize our ability to predict the extent of firms' illegal behavior, the corporate characteristics examined proved not to be strong predictors. Indeed, knowledge of a firm's growth, diversification, and market power added virtually no predictive power when combined with size and financial measures, which were themselves not strong predictors of corporate involvement in illegal activity. Thus, information on firm financial performance and structural characteristics is, by itself, insufficient for explaining corporate crime. . . . A more satisfactory explanation is that economic pressures and other factors operate in a corporate environment that is conducive to unethical and illegal practices. On the other hand, one may find extensive corporate violations where no financial pressures or structural characteristics are evident [Clinard and Yeager, 1980: 132].

On the whole, middle management felt that violations were more likely to arise not from poor financial situations, but from the role of an aggressive "go-go" type of top management, especially the CEO seeking to achieve power and prestige rapidly, both for himself and the corporation. This view is strongly suggested by a number of economic studies in which the importance of profits and market share alone have tended to be minimized as corporate goals; instead, emphasis has been put on multiple goals such as satisfactory growth and increased power and prestige for the corporation (Cyert and March, 1963). In this connection, Galbraith (1971: 174) feels that after a level of satisfactory profitability has been reached, corporate growth may become the primary goal in an attempt to increase opportunities for adding additional personal gain and promotions, which in turn increase the power, prestige, and compensation of top management. One executive recognized the manifold financial goals of a corporation:

> Most of the time the difference is the "bottom line" in order to get profits where pressures are great — either the corporation is

losing money, not getting as much as they want, or they are not getting their proper share of the market.

Other studies, on the other hand, have presented evidence that is directly opposed to the views of the middle management executives. For example, one study that followed 500 large firms over a five-year period found that corporations cited for anti-trust violations prospered less well financially than did other firms (Staw and Szwajkowski, 1975). Similar conclusions were reached by Asch and Seneca (1969). Another, much earlier study by Lane (1953/1977) found firm economic decline to be associated with unfair trade practices in New England's shoe industry. These and other findings have suggested that certain types of corporate violations may reflect general pressure to maximize profits because of financial goal difficulties. Such corporate financial pressures on top management can be great and, as a result, they may face problems in choosing an ethical solution. The president of one large corporation said that the pressures were enormous when things started to go wrong:

> You think, can I do anything about it? Do I screw around with earnings for the quarter and try to cover up and then worry down the road? You feel in a crunch between obligation and reality. You look around and you don't see a way out. When I read the Nixon tapes eight or nine years ago, and read about these meetings about what kind of public image should be presented, well, I've been in meetings like that. The good people, though, test such ideas against morality and legality [Kleinfield, 1982].

Top management appears to emphasize more strongly than middle management the relation of financial factors to unethical and illegal behavior. A study of top management's views found that they considered their primary responsibilities to be their firms' financial interests. They felt that "business executives . . . have no right to wrap themselves in the mantle of moral philosophers and judges — especially to the detriment of the interests of their shareholders whose money they are using" (Silk and Vogel, 1976: 229). A few even argued that "executives' responsibility to the economic survival of institutions sometimes dictated that they violate the law; if they did not, their stockholders would suffer, and other firms 'with less scrupulous management' would win out" (Silk and Vogel, 1976: 228).

Unfair Competitive Practices

Nearly two-thirds of the interviewees believed that the unfair competitive practices of other corporations had little or no effect on the behavior of an ethical corporation; that is, that the unethical corporations largely fail to influence the practices of the ethical ones. Only a small minority felt strongly that corporations must engage in unethical practices in order to remain competitive, and only about one-fifth of the executives were of the opinion that unfair competitive practices constituted a major factor in distinguishing ethical from unethical corporations. In fact, examined in terms of total responses, only about one in seven mentioned such competition at all.

Since little evidence exists as to the overall role of competitive practices in illegal corporate behavior, little can be said to contradict these opinions. Some have maintained, however, that the success of some organizations in the unlawful attainment of their goals encourages others to follow similar paths (Stinchcombe, 1965; Vaughan, 1982: 1385). Competitive practices do play a role in pricefixing violations, with the purpose being to remove the competition and present a situation wherein many corporations may join the conspiracy, largely in self-protection. Pricefixing has been widespread in recent years, and there have been resulting criminal, civil, and administrative prosecutions in a wide variety of industries, including paper products, electrical wiring, apparel, resins used to make paints, crayons, citrus fruits, computers, beer, plywood, armored car services, photography, and toilet seats (Clinard and Yeager, 1980: 141).

When one examines certain industries, on the other hand, a more specific role for competitive practices appears to emerge. Middle management executives mentioned this on several occasions but did not emphasize industry to a great extent. In explaining the reason for some corporations being more ethical than others, only one in ten stated explicitly that this was due to the ethical or unethical practices that tend to characterize certain industries. One executive said: "Violations are characteristic of some industries that are highly competitive, such as the paper industry." Another said: "Some industries such as oil are more given to violations." Pronounced industry differences did emerge indirectly, however, in answer to a number of questions. For example, executives were asked to rate their own industries; although two out of three approved of the ethics of their industries as a whole, about one-third said that their industries rated only fair. Those in the aerospace and motor vehicle industries, particularly, felt that there were numerous unethical and illegal practices within their industries. On the other hand, those in metals (metal manufacturing and metal products) and in chemicals gave their industries a high rating.

In view of the literature in the area, one might have expected middle management to put more stress on the type of industry in which a particular corporation operated. More than thirty years ago, Sutherland (1949: 254) pointed out that violations may result when corporations in an industry face similar economic conditions. Frequently, it is not the internal corporate organization itself that is of importance; rather, it is the corporation's position in the industry (Riedel, 1968: 94). Internal corporate factors may tend to interact with the external situation operating within the industry. As one writer has summarized the situation, the ethical behavior of a corporation is the product of an "ever-shifting pattern of guidelines set by the necessities of the market, the conditions and traditions of the industry, the goals of the corporation, the aspirations of management, and the nature of the executives themselves" (Goodman, 1963: 82).

According to Sutherland (1949: 263), the illegal behavior of a corporation and its executives results from the diffusion of illegal practices and policies within the industry. In a reanalysis of data collected by Sutherland on corporate restraint of trade, Cressey (1976) found that corporations within the same industry generally had similar rates of recidivism. Likewise, a study of pricefixing reported that this offense was more likely to occur when corporations dealt with a homogeneous product line (Hay and Kelley, 1974).

Relatively frequent references were made by the middle management executives to unethical practices in the motor vehicle and oil industries. In a study of Fortune 500 corporate law violations, the motor vehicle, oil, and pharmaceutical industries led all fourteen major industry types in violations and in sanctions imposed (Clinard and Yeager, 1980: 119-122). The motor vehicle industry had 3.9 times its proportionate share of total violations and five times its share of serious and moderately serious violations. The figures for the oil refinery industry were 3.2 and 1.7 times, and for the pharmaceutical industry 2.5 and 3.2 times their proportionate shares of total and of serious and moderately serious violations. Although it was a common practice for large aircraft manufacturers to make questionable and illegal foreign payoffs, the pace was generally believed to have been set by Lockheed, particularly in Japan (Shaplen, 1978). The role of industry ethics is shown particularly in the widespread conspiracy throughout the important carton manufacturing industry that resulted in the indictment of 23 of these concerns and fifty of their executives in 1976 (Clinard and Yeager, 1980: 61-62).

Government Regulation

There are two types of government regulation. There is the older, *economic* regulatory type that sets rates and operating conditions within a given industry — for example, by the Interstate Commerce Commission. These regulations are directed primarily at correcting or offsetting monopoly practices in the free market economy. Second, there is the more recent type of *social* or *protective* regulation. Most regulatory acts of this type came into being because the marketplace and private suits were unable to control conditions that would guarantee worker safety and/or consumer safety, as in foods, drugs, and medical devices; pollution abatement; nondiscrimination; and the control of waste disposal sites. The great increase in protective legislation from the mid-1960s through the 1970s was partially a response to various political action groups.

Ralph Nader's *Unsafe at Any Speed* took on the giant of the automobile industry and the publicity the book received forced the government into taking action to regulate auto safety. Earth Day was the culmination of several years of political mobilization to dramatize how America's rivers were not only devoid of beneficial life and repulsive to our aesthetic senses, but a source of poison and disease. Smog in industrialized regions — and surrounding areas — became a symbol of environmental concern that everyone could understand. Occupational hazards, with effects well beyond the localized ones of mining accidents, were brought to public attention: asbestos and chemicals used in both industry and the home were found to contain carcinogens. It seemed that hardly a day passed without reports of some prospective new source of cancer-causing materials invisibly invading our work places and private lives. Organized political action groups became skillful at

focusing attention on these threats to our lives and society
[Graymer and Thompson, 1982: 11].

In recent years there has been much publicity about government
regulations, along with strong criticism of government protective
regulations, particularly in the business media, by spokesmen for
business and by politicians.[4] Charge have been made that regulatory
agencies are often characterized by the need to eliminate conflicting
rules and regulations within the regulatory process itself, an
overlapping of regulatory jurisdictions, a lack of consideration of the
cost-benefit ratio of the regulatory process, inadequate checks and
balances on the regulatory process, and a failure to concentrate on
business abuses that threaten the public good, as opposed to "trivial"
bureaucratic regulations. It is also claimed that the additional cost of
many government regulations cuts heavily into profits, and that these
are unjustified on a cost-benefit basis.

Many believe, on the other hand, that most government
regulations are necessary to create and develop corporate
responsibility to the public, the government, and competitors. In fact,
many of the charges facing regulatory agencies have been disputed by
others as exaggerations or the result of failing to recognize other
factors. Some have complained, for example, that corporate cost
compliance figures have been greatly magnified. It has even been
claimed that one set of figures may be submitted to the SEC, another
to the public (Green, 1979). One report, issued in 1982, of a three-year
study made by the Conservation Foundation found that the
environmental laws and regulations of the 1970s have not created
insurmountable problems or blocked the construction of new oil
refineries, steel mills, and other industrial plants.[5] The report also
branded as a myth the claim that industries were playing one state off
against another by threatening to locate where environmental laws
were the weakest. Moreover, cost-benefit analysis is difficult to apply
to regulations that prevent the serious injury or death of even a few
workers or consumers. Obviously, many issues are involved, varying
with the type of situations to be regulated and the nature of the
government agency concerned (Argyris et al., 1978; Wilson, 1980;
Bardach and Kagan, 1982; Guzzardi, 1982; and Graymer and
Thompson, 1982).

These types of charges have given the impression that nearly all
government regulations should be abolished and that industry should

be left to regulate itself. In fact, one middle management executive stated: "Management would be more responsible if there were no government regulations. The present situation leaves it up to government to find the violations." It was thus surprising to find that well over half (57.2 percent) of the middle management executives interviewed believed that government regulation is needed and that industry is not able to police itself adequately. If one adds responses that, even with industry self-regulation, "some" government regulation is necessary, the number in favor increased to three out of four. A further indication of their general support for government regulation was the credit given to such agencies as OSHA and the Consumer Product Safety Commission. It was felt that government regulations are needed to assure ethical compliance by others in the industry and to guarantee worker and consumer safety, for example. Some stated that government regulations are often brought on by unethical business practices in the industry, and since at least some government regulation is perceived to be necessary, over half took the position that the presence of government does not, in itself, contribute to an atmosphere conducive to violation. Only one in seven thought that government regulation produces much of this type of effect. Difficulties in complying with one government regulation do not always produce an attitude of noncompliance with others.

The views of middle management about the necessity for basic government regulation of industry coincided with those of a sample of top executives of Fortune 500 corporations who had been interviewed confidentially (Clinard and Yeager, 1980: 99-100). One executive said: "We must have government regulation; without them we would have to pay too high a price for safety and [risk] the pollution of the environment." Another said that such regulations "set the basic rules of the game; without them there would be chaos in the corporate world. The very existence of government regulations indicates the possibility that if corporations are not more honest there will be more regulations." A senior executive of one large corporation stated that there is "much greed in business and consequently it is impossible to do away with government regulations. The role of the federal government in policing corporations is a proper one, for if each state wrote its own regulations it would be chaos nationally." All of them agreed, of course, like middle management, that government regulation is sometimes carried too far. In a larger study, similar views were expressed by the top management of the Fortune 500, nearly all of whom were agreed on the need for newer protective government agencies (Silk and Vogel, 1976: 53).

Considerable support for the views of both middle and top management can also be found in studies made of the problems of government regulation. One of the most critical discussions of government regulatory agencies stated at the outset:

> Few could seriously contend in our modern technological society that the government should not provide reasonable protection against securities fraud or guard against pricefixing and unreasonable restraints of trade. Nor could the government abandon machinery for the orderly process of collective bargaining [Stokes, 1982: ix].

Another volume on government regulations, co-edited by the President of Atlantic Richfield, stated in the introduction:

> Business may chafe under the restraints and expense of the regulatory process, but the plain fact is that regulation is a less harmful way to inject the public interest into private institutions than the likeliest alternatives, those largely associated with the overall planning of authoritarian states. Consumer interests, environmental protection, health, and safety all require standards, and standards require monitoring. Thus, regulation grows with every extension of the public interest [Bradshaw and Vogel, 1981: xxiv].

A recent book dealing with reforming social regulation concluded that "public support for maintaining a cleaner and safer environment remains strong" (Graymer and Thompson, 1982: 16). Irving Shapiro (1981: 215), Chairman of the Board and Chief Executive Officer of DuPont, in an article on occupational health and safety, has stated: "Certainly we need laws on the books covering safety and health, and we need inspection provisions to ensure that those laws are being carried out." Others have said that "government regulation has become necessary because of the failure of industry to provide willingly for the health, safety, and well-being of the public, consumers, and workers" (Clinard and Yeager, 1980: 214).

Where business ethics have been weak, and the contradiction with profits great, the government has had to step into corporate affairs, albeit sometimes too vigorously. The forces that have shaped government intervention and regulation, however, are complex and are the result of conflicting forces and interest groups — what has been termed the "politics of regulation" (Weaver, 1978; Wilson, 1980; Barnett, 1981; Kahn, 1982). A professor of business administration has perhaps best summarized the realities of government regulation, in a sense summarizing the prevailing views of middle management executives:

> The most controversial dimension of corporate social performance involves business-government relations. Mainstream corporate opinion has become highly critical of government regulation. It is blamed for promoting inflation, retarding technological innovation, reducing productivity, and increasing economic concentration. This perspective, however, is not shared by all corporate executives. There is recognition on the part of some members of the business community that regulations are attempting, however imperfectly, to address real social problems and that much of the pressure for increased regulation is in response to previous corporate abuses. Rather than automatically oppose any new regulation, those executives have instead sought to promote constructive alternatives. Accepting the goals of regulation, they then seek to draw upon their own experience to offer suggestions about how it can be made more effective. Still others have engaged in voluntary efforts to improve the quality of public debate about business-government relations [Vogel, 1981: xi].

Industry Self-Regulation

The majority of middle management executives pointed out that industry cannot police itself effectively without some government intervention. In their opinions, the unethical behavior of certain top management personnel within an industry, plus the greed and unethical practices of some corporations, have made government regulation necessary. Moreover, they could visualize no way in which industry rules might be effectively enforced.

The views of these middle management executives seem to be in accord with most of the persons who have studied regulation, namely, that social control measures should largely constitute a complementary, rather than a competitive, relationship between industry and government. Similarly, in a survey of thirteen large corporations, two out of three top executives, and 58 percent of middle management executives, felt that their corporations generally seek to work cooperatively with government agencies (Cox, 1982: 233). A good example of this followed the well-publicized case of cyanide-laced Extra-Strength Tylenol capsules, sold over the counter, that resulted in several deaths in late 1982. The association of nonprescription drug manufacturers immediately asked for the quick acceptance by the FDA of its proposed broad national standards that would require tamper-resistant packaging for over-the-counter medicines. As the senior vice president of the association said: "It is rare for an industry of this size, one with about $6 billion a year in sales, to ask for more regulation" (The Wall Street Journal, October 15, 1982).

Under what conditions might a voluntary self-regulation system work? One writer who has carefully examined self-regulation concluded that it might work if certain industry conditions existed: (1) broad social consensus on programmatic goals, as has occurred in various areas of food and drug regulation; (2) the existence of administrative and technical skills in monitoring self-regulatory arrangements, both in industry and through help from the government; (3) the availability of technical knowledge and skills to produce an ethical product in firms and industries; (4) the readiness to cope with political opposition from firms within the industry that benefit from the existing regulatory situation; and (5) the willingness and ability of regulatory agencies to deal effectively with the "bad apples," even while letting up on the "good apples," and the "readiness on the part of consumer organizations and others to give industry voluntarism a fair hearing" (Grumbly, 1982: 115-117). A related but different proposal is that of "enforced self-regulation" at the corporation level. Braithwaite (1982: 1503) has explained such a proposal this way:

> Under enforced self-regulation, each company would write its own rules. Once these rules had been ratified by the government, a violation of them would be an offense. The company would be required to establish an internal compliance group to monitor observance of the rules and recommend disciplinary action against violators. If management were to fail to rectify violations or to act on recommendations for disciplinary action, the director of compliance would be statutorily required to report this fact to the relevant agency. The role of the regulatory agency would be to

determine that the company rules satisfied all of the guidelines set down by government policy, to ensure that the compliance group was independent within the corporate bureaucracy, to audit the performance of the compliance group, to conduct occasional spot inspections of operating units as an independent check that the compliance unit was detecting violations, and to launch prosecutions, particularly against companies that subverted their compliance groups.

On the other hand, nearly all middle management executives expressed the view that government regulation has been carried too far and that some reduction in the number of rules and requirements is needed. They pointed out that many regulations are too complex to be thoroughly understood and that many are not only unrealistic but unfair. Top executives also believe that regulation has often become excessive and is formulated with little understanding of economic costs (Silk and Vogel, 1976: 53). As one executive said: "I spend too much time complying with government regulations." Another said that "EPA is an absolute necessity. Yet as we are making progress [in compliance], it is growing."

Those who have studied the regulatory problem have suggested that government regulation tends to become excessive when (1) compliance would not materially reduce the harms in question, (2) compliance would produce benefits only at a disproportionately large cost, and (3) less costly alternative requirements would be of comparable effectiveness (Bardach and Kagan, 1982: 10). A recent survey of social regulation concluded that the methods used to deal with the problems are "often inappropriate, frequently contradictory, and fail to achieve goals in the most efficient manner" (Graymer and Thompson, 1982: 14).

Responsibility for promoting a cleaner, safer, healthier environment has been concentrated in the hands of regulatory officials who have frequently failed to consider alternatives to uniform application of design standards or to command-and-control types of regulation. More often than not the approaches chosen or required by law have failed to target monitoring and enforcement activities where they would have the greatest payoff. Regulators are generally more attentive to those who benefit from the agency's activities than to those who are likely to be harmed [Graymer and Thompson, 1982: 265].

IMPLICATIONS FOR SOCIAL CONTROL

The middle management executives had spent most of their working lives in the world of the Fortune 500; they had been associated with a single corporation for an average of 32 years. With this background, one cannot take lightly their opinions as to why some corporations break the law more often than others, nor their specific suggestions for controlling unethical and illegal corporate behavior.

According to them, the mere presence of possible government enforcement action appears to have served as a deterrent to many unethical and illegal actions. In this connection, several spoke of the importance of "government looking over the corporation's shoulder." According to the executives, this is particularly true in the case of corporations that depend largely on government contracts and where possible government enforcement actions might preclude their obtaining future contracts. This view, of course, depends on the corporation's belief that government agencies have the will, the budget, and the staffs to enforce regulations. In practice, this has not been the case in recent years (Clinard and Yeager, 1980: 95-96, 315-316). Certainly this was not the case in the early 1980s, when the agencies that regulate corporate behavior experienced drastically reduced budgets, all of which were already extremely inadequate. For example, Stanley Sporkin, former SEC enforcement chief, commented in 1982 on the SEC's more lenient attitude toward corporate violations: "When you get headlines that say 'SEC to Limit Pursuit of Unethical Conduct' as recently appeared in *The Washington Post*, that perception is troublesome" (The Wall Street Journal, December 27, 1982).

Top Management

For the most part, enforcement efforts should clearly be directed at top management, as it is they who carry the responsibility for much illegal behavior and who generally, in the opinion of middle management, know about important violations, either before or not long after they occur. Various studies have shown that fines imposed on corporations have far less deterrent effect than do enforcement actions against top executives, as, for example, a criminal proceeding (see Clinard and Yeager, 1980: 280-298). Corporate fines are often treated as the cost of doing business, whereas corporate executives fear the stigma associated with a criminal conviction; above all, they fear the possibility of imprisonment (Geis, 1972). In fact, several middle management executives went further, pointing out that it is the presence of government regulations, and possible enforcement actions in general, that tends to keep top management in line.[6]

Actions against top management present many problems, due to the hierarchical nature of the corporate structure. When offenses are committed in a corporate context, individual executive responsibility is hard to assign. It is not an easy task for enforcement staff to determine where the responsibility and the authority to insure compliance with a specific law or regulation lie, so great is the diversification and so complicated the power structure of any large corporation. To have any chance of success in an enforcement action, a top executive's responsibility for it must be proved, along with the authority resting with him to prevent or correct an alleged violation. Often, top executives argue, they cannot be held responsible for acts they did not authorize and about which they had no specific knowledge. Such a defense is fostered in the corporate environment in the sense that middle management might often know what top management wants of them without their having to ask.

Deterrent Effect of Enforcement Actions

According to several executives, the ethical patterns within a corporation or within an industry were improved and maintained where the government had taken strong enforcement actions in the past. A number of them, for example, pointed out the continuing effects of pricefixing and antimonopoly enforcement actions brought by the government years ago. Support for this view comes from a study of criminal anti-trust prosecutions in the bread industry which had significant subsequent deterrent effects on pricefixing (Block et al., 1981). The degree of deterrence was surprising in that none of the executives went to jail. In this case, deterrence was strengthened by private civil damage suits that followed in the wake of criminal prosecution. Moreover, prior enforcement actions, according to the executives, had not only affected compliance in the particular area in which they were brought, but also had tended to affect compliance with government regulations generally. Surveying the evidence, two writers in the area of corporate crime have concluded that deterrence is quite effective, particularly with specific corporations or in the case of executives who have been prosecuted successfully (Braithwaite and Geis, 1982).

Consent Orders

In a consent agreement, the corporation reaches an understanding with the government not to violate the law or regulation again. This agreement is ratified by the court in the case of a consent decree. On a number of occasions, middle management executives mentioned the continuing effect on compliance of a consent agreement or decree imposed long ago on their own corporations or on several corporations within the industry, including their own. According to them, the corporation's wishes were to avoid additional judicial proceedings or the adverse publicity that would develop should they again violate the law.

This view does not agree with the general view that severely criticizes the extensive use by the government of consent agreements and decrees in cases of corporate violation. In cases of conventional crime, plea bargaining may be used, but there is nothing comparable to a consent decree. Thus, many regard its use for corporations as a mere "slap on the wrist," with little real enforcement effect. Middle management, on the other hand, pointed out that such actions force corporations to "shape up," as they put it. As one executive said: "The consent decree forced us to shape up. Twice a year our officials met with the U.S. Department of Justice officials to see if we were in any violation." Moreover, on numerous occasions middle management mentioned the fears their corporations had of individual or class action consumer suits. Such suits could not only be far more costly than a government administrative or civil monetary penalty (or a corporate fine, in a criminal case), but they could result in adverse publicity.

Prevention

Obviously, the most satisfactory and effective approach to corporate unethical practices and illegalities is the prevention of these activities, rather than after-the-fact enforcement actions. Scattered throughout the comments of the middle management executives were corporate practices that they felt to be important in accomplishing this objective; many of them are worthy of consideration. Among the more ethical corporations were the following practices:

(1) strong controls over corporate ethics on the part of top management, in which the need to uphold the reputation and the brand names of the corporation are stressed;

(2) frequent guidelines on regulations from top management, particularly on new regulations. Top management would spell out how the corporation is affected and why there is a need for the corporation to comply;

(3) quarterly staff meetings for middle management, including plant managers, together with top management, in which new regulations and problems of compliance are discussed at both top and middle management levels;

(4) an open-door policy involving a specific request from top management that middle management consult with them about problems of ethics and compliance with government regulations;

(5) middle managment discussions with the corporate legal staff who frequently visit the plant or divisions;

(6) frequent visits from the home office to plants and subsidiaries in order to check on compliance with government regulations;

(7) specific training programs for middle management in the areas of ethics and government regulations;

(8) requesting all middle management to sign a statement each year indicating their familiarity with all pertinent government regulations;

(9) requesting all middle management executives to sign a paper indicating that they knew they would be fired if there were violations; and

(10) penalties such as dismissal to prevent middle managers from violating government regulations.

These ideas indicate the crucial role of actions by top management in preventing unethical corporate practices and violations, a position supported in a study of the views of top management of many of the

Fortune 500 corporations. "Many business executives felt that the only way to deal with the problem of stopping dishonest or illegal corporate behavior was for top management itself to adopt high standards, make these crystal clear to everyone below them, and then lay down the line in unmistakable terms" (Silk and Vogel, 1976: 225). One top executive stated: "The heads of the institutions set the tone for their organization. We are not adequately insisting on morality from the top" (Silk and Vogel, 1976: 221).

Others suggested how the very nature of corporate organization can affect the control of unethical and illegal behavior. Their views about the necessity for top management continuously to inspect the corporation for compliance with ethics and regulations agrees with that of top management (Silk and Vogel, 1976: 226):

Smaller corporate divisions facilitate better control over unethical and illegal practices.[7]

The location of the corporate home office in a smaller community makes it more difficult to conceal unethical or illegal practices. Furthermore, the reputation of the corporation in the community is more important.[8]

Having audit committees on the board of directors make closer checks on accounting practices and compliance with government regulations.

The regular use of internal operational financial auditors to make it easier to detect violations like illegal marketing, payoffs, and kickbacks. Also of great usefulness is the wider use of quality control inspectors.

The exchange of information with competitors on their efforts to comply with employee health and safety regulations and pollution controls, as well as in aiding compliance generally.

Sending corporation representatives to Washington to discuss the purposes of the regulations, as well as the problems associated with compliance. Furthermore, as one executive put it, "we could then find out where we failed and how this made a government regulation necessary."

The Reporting of Violations by Employees

Corporate violations become known to a government agency through many sources: consumer complaints, government investigations, customers, competitors, the press, and present or former employees, including executives. A controversial issue in this matter is whether or not a corporate employee should go to the government about serious violations of regulations when the corporation itself, including top management, has done nothing about them. For example, two employees involved in the falsification of test data on airplane brakes were promoted by their companies, while two other workers who brought the falsified data and information on the dangers involved to the attention of government officials found themselves forced to resign (Vandivier, 1972).

Some persons believe that employees should not only inform the government, but that they should be given protection by law so that their positions remain no different from that of a citizen who has informed the police about an ordinary crime (see, for example, Nader et al., 1976). Precedents for doing so now exist in the government. Under the Nixon Administration, for example, a ranking Defense Department employee testified before Congress about cost overruns that had been concealed from Congress on a defense project; he was subsequently fired on orders from above. Some years later he was reinstated with back pay. In corporate business, however, one can encounter cases such as the following: According to *Time* magazine (April 17, 1972), a former chairman of General Motors asserted that "some enemies of business" now even encourage employees to be disloyal and that whatever label is attached to such practices, "industrial espionage, whistle-blowing or professional responsibility, it is another tactic for spreading disunity and creating conflict."

In this connection, three out of four middle management executives felt, however, that corporate employees should be protected by the government from dismissal should they report a serious violation. They felt that employees should be able to go to the government without fear of dismissal and should not be penalized for doing what they believe is important and right — providing, of course, that their actions are not precipitated by a grudge against the corporation. One out of four recognized, however, that, although their positions would be protected, their continued association with the corporation would be difficult.

A large proportion of top executives appear to have views on this question that are similar to the views of middle management. For example, one study revealed an increasing acceptance of the rights of employees by business people, particularly in the area of whistle-blowing. Of those executives surveyed, 61 percent agreed that if a whistle-blower sincerely believes that he or she is acting in the best interests of the customers, the stockholders, or the community, the person should not be penalized (Ewing, 1977). Only one-third of them felt that if a whistle-blower does not like the company he or she should leave; less than one-tenth felt that the whistle-blower should be penalized if there is "factual evidence that the whistle blower is hurting sales" (Ewing, 1977: 91). One writer has pointed out, however, that such employee rights touch a sensitive issue in corporations: "When critics claim that workers have rights to blow the whistle . . . the executives may reply that talk of employee rights is merely a camouflaged attempt to rob individuals and corporations of rightful authority and that it will breed chaos and inefficiency" (Donaldson, 1982: 136).

Opinions of middle management executives about the question of reporting serious violations to the government varied according to the type of violation: it was assumed in each case that corporate channels had been exhausted. An overwhelming support was shown for reporting worker safety violations (OSHA), about which middle management felt strongly. In fact, some stated that it would be unethical not to report them, as it might endanger lives or cause injury to others. On the other hand, for different reasons, they felt just as strongly that employees, including middle management, should not report to the government violations such as pricefixing, illegal rebates and kickbacks, and illegal payments to foreign officials. Although they gave various reasons for not reporting these violations (for example, pricefixing, illegal rebates, and kickbacks are not the concern of middle management, and foreign payoffs are customary ways of doing business in some countries), the general theme throughout was that to do so would be disloyal to the corporation. Such employees (some even felt this way about worker safety) would be disloyal and should leave the corporation if they felt strongly enough about the matter.

In conclusion, government agencies cannot depend to any marked degree on corporate employees as a source for ascertaining the existence of many serious corporate violations. Other sources of information must be used, which obviously makes the enforcement picture even more complicated. Although employee protection against dismissal by the government might encourage some personnel to report violations, this protection would probably not affect the situation markedly.

NOTES

1. This comprehensive study of corporate control and corporate power was made under the auspices of the Twentieth Century Fund.

2. The fifteen corporations that they cited primarily were the following: Bechtel, Boeing, Caterpillar, Dana, Delta Airlines, Digital Equipment, Emerson Electric, Fluor, Hewlett-Packard, IBM, Johnson & Johnson, McDonald's, Procter & Gamble, Texas Instruments, and 3M.

3. This survey was based on a lengthy mailed questionnaire that involved responses from 555 top and 571 middle management corporate executives. Although all of the corporations were large, there were only thirteen, and of these only four were in the Fortune 500. Four were service corporations like the Hyatt Hotels, and some "consumer" corporations like the Encyclopedia Brittanica and Taft Broadcasting. With such a small and diverse sample, and with the analysis limited to only two groups (top and middle management), it is impossible to reach many valid conclusions from the survey. No questions were asked about the executives' views of corporate ethics or about violations (Cox, 1982).

4. A 1981 Gallup Poll conducted for the League of Women Voters revealed that the U.S. public does not even know what "government regulations" are, with more than half not knowing the difference between a government law and a regulation, nearly one-half believing they were drafted by Congress, and one-half being unable to name a federal regulation that affected them or their family.

5. This foundation, established in 1948, is a nonprofit environmental research organization that receives financial support from private foundations, corporations, and individuals.

6. Today, community service is a commonly used sanction against corporations and their executives as an alternative to imprisonment. There are arguments for and against such a sanction. It is increasingly, but still rarely, being employed for ordinary offenders as well (Fisse, 1981).

7. A similar conclusion was reached in a study of the fifteen best-run large U.S. corporations (Peters and Waterman, 1982). Corporations are broken into small independent units; they will build a new factory in a different city rather than expand an existing site.

8. Lane (1953/1977: 109) found support for this in that differences in violations of law among New England show manufacturing concerns were closely linked to community attitudes "towards the law, the government, and the morality of illegality."

APPENDIX A

Locating the Sample

Our original assumption was that it would be simple to identify retired Fortune 500 middle management executives and then to select a sample randomly. It was known that there is no roster of retired Fortune 500 executives, such as might be expected for high-ranking military officers; it was also realized that it would not be feasible to write to a large number of corporations to request the names and present addresses of their retired executives. Instead, major reliance was to be placed on the membership roster of SCORE (Service Corps of Retired Executives) and on such service organizations as Rotary. SCORE is a national organization that consists of some 10,000 retired business people, whose purpose it is to furnish management and technical advice to owners/managers of small businesses who request management counseling.

Although SCORE is a totally independent organization, it is sponsored by the Small Business Administration of the U.S. Department of Commerce. This source did not prove to be useful in locating interviewees, for a variety of reasons; in fact, only seven out of a final sample of 64 executives were obtained through SCORE. First of all, the Small Business Administration could not furnish the membership roster of selected SCORE chapters, a decision left to individual chapters. Second, although the Santa Fe SCORE chapter (the city in which the researcher resides), which was contacted early in designing the study, had a considerable proportion of Fortune 500 executives, this did not turn out to be the case for the other SCORE chapters that were canvassed. Third, SCORE chapters located in retirement communities have small memberships due to the limited number of small business concerns within these areas. Fourth, access to membership rosters is entirely up to each chapter. Also of little value in the search for interviewees were Rotary clubs. Only one interview was obtained through this source, even though several Rotary clubs in the Phoenix and Tucson areas were contacted. Most Rotary club members appeared to be from small local businesses rather than from large corporations like the Fortune 500. Managers of Fortune 500 plants or subsidiaries located in a community, however, were frequently members of service clubs.

For these reasons, therefore, the identification of a sample became one of the major problems of the study. Since SCORE had to be largely abandoned as a source, it was concluded that there were only two other means of locating an interview sample — the use of retirement community directories and referrals from persons already interviewed. It was discovered, fortunately, that both Sun City, a retirement community of 58,000 persons in the Phoenix suburbs, and Green Valley, a community of retirees (16,000 population) south of Tucson, publish community telephone directories that list previous business affiliations or other occupations under the person's name. Thus it seemed possible to identify easily those middle management executives who had last worked for one of the Fortune 500 corporations. Concentrating interviews in these two retirement areas had the additional advantage of making it possible to secure other persons through referrals from executives previously interviewed, since they were likely to have a wide acquaintanceship in the community.

In view of the frequency of the listing of Fortune 500 corporations in the directories, and our awareness of the general affluence of these two Arizona retirement communities, it was anticipated that a fairly large number of middle management executives would be available for interviewing. This did not turn out to be the case; it was learned by telephoning that the majority of those who listed a corporate affiliation had not been in middle management. Instead, many had been supervisors and a few, top managers. In the case of supervisory staff it was sometimes even difficult to get through to a prospective interviewee due to the fact that when the wife of a supervisor, for example, answered the phone she often requested, now and then in an officious manner, a complete explanation of the purpose of the call, something that never happened when wives of the middle management executives answered. In some calls that revealed that the corporate affiliation was that of supervisor, a certain degree of hostility toward middle management was revealed. One person who had been a supervisor said: "I was in middle management for two years and got out of that." Another said: "I was not in that stuff" and hung up.

A great many long distance calls were made to locate persons who had been in middle management positions. The selection of persons from the community directories was entirely at random: Sun City calls were made to listings under A, B, H, S, and T; Green Valley names were randomly selected from A to M. Successful interview arrangements represented 16.4 percent of all calls, or 6.5 per interview. In addition to finding that the person had not been in middle management, the calls were often otherwise unproductive. Often the person had not been in the proper middle management category, had been retired more than ten years, was too ill to talk or had died, or was not allowed by his wife to talk. There were also cases where no replies were received after several calls were made, and a few refusals were encountered (see Table A-1).

It was necessary at the outset of each call to explain fully the purpose and nature of the call prior to making an inquiry about the nature of the person's corporate affiliation. Without this explanation, a potential middle management interviewer might have been lost had the person hung up or immediately declined, or if the researcher had simply asked, at the outset: "Were you in middle management?" This careful explanation required several minutes, during which it was stated that the call was long distance, giving the researcher's name and his previous affiliation with the University of Wisconsin; that he had previously interviewed a number of top management executives in an earlier study and was now making a study of middle management; that both the name of the person, as well as any specific reference to his corporation, would remain confidential; that the questions dealt, for example, with corporate ethics, pressures on middle management, and attitudes toward regulations; and that the interviews were to be conducted in a hotel room where privacy could be assured. Occasionally, although not frequently, a number of questions were asked by potential middle management interviewees before they agreed to be

TABLE A-1   Results of Phone Calls Using Sun City and Green Valley Community Directories

	Number	Percentage
Not middle management (supervisors)	73	37.5
Not middle management (top management)	5	2.5
Middle management but not in chosen categories (specialist, research, plant facilities, or construction)	5	2.5
Retired more than ten years	19	9.7
Deceased	20	10.3
Moved, phone disconnected, and so forth	12	6.2
Too ill or wife would not permit him to talk	8	4.1
No answer (after two or three calls)	12	6.2
Refusals by middle management	9	4.6
Interviews arranged from directories	32	16.4
Total	195	100.0

interviewed. Among these questions were queries about the purpose of the study, who was supporting it, whether complete anonymity could really be assured (some were concerned about their corporate pensions), where the results of the study might be published, and what assurances could be given that their answers would be useful in view of the fact that they were retired from the corporation, most of them for several years.

Referrals

At the conclusion of the interview, each person was asked for help in obtaining the names of other potential interviewees. It was pointed out that with the use of directories, many telephone calls had to be made to obtain the names of persons who fit the sample and who were willing to be interviewed. Respondents were given a list of the Fortune 500 corporations over the past five years, as many of these corporations are not well known. In addition, nearly all interviews were followed by a letter thanking the interviewee for his cooperation and including this statement: "The most difficult problem I have encountered has been to locate retired middle management (retired ten years or less) persons of the Fortune 500 corporations. If you should know of other persons I should greatly appreciate your sending me their names, the corporate affiliation, and the phone numbers. As indicated to you, I do not attribute anything anyone says either by name or by corporation."

Of the 64 persons in the sample, 21 were obtained through a referral by someone who had been interviewed, and three from names furnished by other persons in the community, for a total of 24, or 37.5 percent. This represents a substantial part of the sample, but it was disappointing in that it had been hoped that more could be obtained through referral. If an average of at least one referral had come from each person interviewed, a much larger sample could have been obtained. Of those whose names had been obtained through referrals, only one did not agree to be interviewed. In most cases, the use of someone else's name was a powerful factor in arranging an interview. More names were actually referred than could be used, however, as a number of them did not meet the sample criteria. Obviously, there was a tendency to refer persons from one's own corporation, since one generally knew them, sometimes through regular meetings of corporate retirees residing in the area. The general rule was not to use more than two interviewees with the same corporate affiliation, although in the case of three corporations, three retirees were used. In the case of several corporations, at least five additional interviews for each corporation could have been used. Others referred persons who, as it turned out, were in top management or in a particular area of middle management not included in the sample. Several referred persons were found to have been retired more than ten years and thus were not within the sample criteria. Two had been with a large corporation not in the Fortune 500, and one had been with a corporation that was a subsidiary of a large foreign corporation.

The underlying reason for not securing the expected number of referrals can only be a matter of speculation. Some interviewees may have been disturbed by the nature of the interview, others might have felt reluctant to involve others in the study, and a few were probably well intentioned but for various reasons did not follow through on the suggestion. Still, many did come through this source, thus reducing the time and effort that would have otherwise been necessary through the laborious use of a community directory. Although a vigorous effort was made to obtain referrals through this means, more could have been done. If, for example, telephone calls had been made later to those who had been interviewed to remind them of the need for additional names, considerably more referrals might have been obtained.

The final sample of 64, therefore, was obtained from a number of sources. SCORE membership rosters accounted for 7 (10.9 percent), Rotary for one (0.3 percent), community directories 32 (50.0 percent), and referrals — that is, other names suggested by those who had been interviewed — 24 (37.5 percent). The fact that referrals turned out to be a useful source indicated something of the success of the original interview.

Some refusals had been anticipated, particularly since the request was being made over the phone by a complete stranger. Moreover, the persons to be interviewed had been executives of considerable status and had to protect their corporate relations and their pensions. Also, many would be concerned about anonymity. However, only ten persons (nine from the community directories and one referral) who met the sample criteria refused to be interviewed. Of this number, two had full-time jobs, although they had been retired from their corporations. Thus, these could not truly be called direct refusals. The five others gave reasons that, on the surface at least, appeared not to involve an unwillingness to be interviewed for any substantive reasons. They simply said: "I play a lot of golf and have no time," "I have no time because of personal problems," "I have no time because I am too involved in community activities," or "I have been away from the corporation too long." One declined, after some probing, saying simply: "I do not see anything in it for me," which meant, presumably, that when he gave time for an interview it might lead to some compensation or a job, or that he did not see any enjoyment in return for the time he would give. Of the remaining eight, three gave no reason except that they did not want to be interviewed.

APPENDIX B

FORTUNE 500 CORPORATIONS WITH WHICH INTERVIEWERS LAST ASSOCIATED

Alcoa
Allis-Chalmers
American Can
Armco Steel
Atlantic Richfield
Bendix
Boeing
Borg-Warner
Burroughs
Caterpillar Tractor
Continental Oil
Dart
Dow Chemical
DuPont
Eaton
FMC
Firestone Tire and Rubber
Ford Motor Co.
General Motors
Gillette
B. F. Goodrich
Goodyear Tire and Rubber
Hobart
Hoerner Waldorf
International Business Machines
International Harvester

Jones and Laughlin
Lockheed
Martin Marietta
McDonnell Douglas
Minnesota Mining and Minerals
Mobil Oil
Monsanto
Pennwalt
Procter and Gamble
Ralston Purina
RCA
Republic Steel
Rockwell International
Schlitz Brewing
Sherwin-Williams
Sperry Rand
Standard Oil of California
Standard Oil of Indiana (AMCO)
Sterling Drug
Texaco
Timken
United Brands
U.S. Gypsum
Westinghouse Electric
White Consolidated Industries

APPENDIX C

TITLE OF LAST POSITION HELD IN CORPORATION AND LOCATION

Marketing

Manager, Marketing Support (Home)
Operations Manager (Western Europe)
Systems Engineer Coordinating with Marketing (Branch)
General Manager, Marketing (Home)
District Sales Manager (Branch) (2)
Regional Marketing Manager (Branch)
Manager, Business Practices (Home)
Chief Engineer Diesel Design, Division (Home)
Manager, Automotive Marketing Division (Home)
Director, Business Development (Subsidiary)
Manager, Western Division Marketing (Subsidiary)
District Manager, Sales Division (Branch)
Sales Manager, Parts Division (Home)
Manager, Advanced Engineering Facilities (Subsidiary)
    (tied to Marketing)
Director, Engineering (Home) (tied to Marketing)
Manager, Agricultural Relations (Home)
Manager, International Division (Home)
Marketing Manager, European Division (Branch)
National Accounts Manager, Division (Home)

Division Sales Manager (Branch)
Executive Vice-President, International Production and
    Marketing Division (Home)
Manager, Wholesale Department (Branch)
Operations Manager, Division (Home)
Manager, International Marketing Division (Branch)

Manufacturing

Plant Manager (Branch) (4)
Production Director (Subsidiary)
Senior Process Engineer (Home)
Production Process Engineer, Division (Home)
Vice-President, Manufacturing Division (Home)
Supervisor, Technical Service (Branch)
Manager of Operations (Branch)
Manager, Manufacturing Facility Planning (Home)
Production Manager (Branch)
Factory Manager, Division (Home)
General Manager, Division (Home)
Assistant Superintendent, Division (Branch)
Manager, Recording Development (Branch)
Division Manager (Branch)
Materials Manager (Branch)
Assistant to Vice-President Manufacturing, Division (Home)
Manager, Systems Management (Branch)

Finance/Accounting

Assistant Treasurer (Home)
Cost Accountant, Special Products Division (Branch)
Supervisor, Employee Benefits Plans (Home)
Budget Coordinator (Branch)
Director, Corporate Taxes (Home)

Other

Manager, Employee Benefits (Home)

Director, Research Administration (Home)
Assistant Manager, Corporate Labor Relations (Home)
General Counsel (Home)
Associate Director, Research and Development (Home)
Director, Corporate Services (Home)
Advanced Design Engineer (Home)
Director, Public Relations (Home)
Manager, Public Relations (Home)
Labor Relations and Personnel Administrator, Division (Home)
Manager, International and Government Relations (Home)
General Purchasing Agent (Home)
Contract Estimator (Home)

BIBLIOGRAPHY

ARGYRIS, C., A.L. CHICKERING, P.H. FELDMAN, R.H. HOLTON, D.P. JACOBS, A.E. KAHN, P.W. MacAVOY, A. PHILLIPS, V.K. SMITH, P.H. WEAVER, and R.J. ZECKHAUSER (1978) Regulating Business: The Search for an Optimum. San Francisco: Institute for Contemporary Studies.

ASCH, P. and J.J. SENECA (1969) "Is collusion profitable?" Review of Economics and Statistics 58 (February): 1-12.

AUBERT, V. (1952/1977) "White-collar crime and social structure," pp. 168-180 in G. Geis and R.F. Meier (eds.) White-Collar Crime (rev. ed.). New York: Free Press.

BARAK-GLANTZ, I.L. and C.R. HUFF [eds.] (1981) The Mad, the Bad, and the Different: Essays in Honor of Simon Dinitz. Lexington, MA: Lexington Books.

BARBER, R.J. (1970) The American Corporation: Its Power, Its Money, Its Politics. New York: E.P. Dutton.

BARDACH, E. and R.A. KAGAN [eds.] (1982) Social Relations: Strategies for Reform. San Francisco: Institute for Contemporary Studies.

BARNET, R. and R. MILLER (1974) Global Reach: The Power of the Multinational Corporation. New York: Simon & Schuster.

BARNETT, H.C. (1981) "Corporate capitalism, corporate crime." Crime and Delinquency (January): 4-23.

BAUMHART, R.C. (1961) "How ethical are businessmen?" Harvard Business Review 39 (July-August): 6-19, 156-176.

BLOCK, M.K., F.C. NOLD, and J.G. SIDAK (1981) "The deterrent effect of antitrust enforcement." Journal of Political Economy (June): 429-445.

BRADSHAW, T. and D. VOGEL [eds.] (1981) Corporations and Their Critics. New York: McGraw-Hill.

BRAITHWAITE, J. (1982) "Enforced self-regulation: a new strategy for corporate crime control." Michigan Law Review 80: 1466-1507.

——— (1979) "Transnational corporations and corruption: towards some international solutions." International Journal of the Sociology of Law 7: 125-142.

177

────── and G. GEIS (1982) "On theory and action for corporate crime control." Crime and Delinquency (April): 292-314.

BRENNER, S. N. and E. A. MOLANDER (1977) "Is the ethics of business changing?" Harvard Business Review 55 (January-February): 57-71.

Business Week (1982) "The boom in executive self-interest." May 24, pp. 16, 20.

────── (1976) "The law closes in on managers." May 10, pp. 110-117.

────── (1975) "Price-fixing: crackdown underway." June 2, pp. 42-49.

CARROLL, A. B. (1975) "Managerial ethics: a post-Watergate view." Business Horizons 18: 75-80.

CLARK, J. P. and R. C. HOLLINGER (1982) Theft by Employees in Work Organizations. Washington, DC: National Institute of Justice.

────── (1977) "On the feasibility of empirical studies of white-collar crime," in R. F. Meier (ed.) Theory in Criminology: Contemporary Views. Beverly Hills, CA: Sage.

CLIFFORD, W. and J. BRAITHWAITE (1981) Cost-Effective Business Regulation: Views From the Australian Business Elite. Canberra: Australian Institute of Criminology.

CLINARD, M. B. (1952) The Black Market: A Study of White Collar Crime. New York: Holt, Rinehart & Winston.

────── and R. QUINNEY (1973) Criminal Behavior Systems: A Typology. New York: Holt, Rinehart & Winston.

CLINARD, M. B. and P. C. YEAGER (1980) Corporate Crime. New York: Free Press.

────── (1979) "Corporate crime: issues in research," in E. Sagarin (ed.) Criminology: New Concerns. Beverly Hills, CA: Sage.

────── J. M. BRISSETTE, D. PETRASHEK, and E. HARRIES (1979) Illegal Corporate Behavior, Washington, DC: Government Printing Office.

Compensation Review (1976) "How companies set the base salary and incentive bonus opportunity for chief-executive and chief-operating officers — a compensation review symposium." Vol. 8, pp. 12-32.

COOPER, M. R., P. A. GELFOND, and P. M. FOLEY (1980) "Early warning signals — growing discontent among managers." Business 30 (January-February): 2-12.

COX, A. (1982) The Cox Report on the American Corporation. New York: Delacorte.

CRESSEY, D. R. (1976) "Restraint of trade, recidivism, and delinquent neighborhoods," in J. F. Short, Jr. (ed.) Delinquency, Crime, and Society. Chicago: University of Chicago Press.

────── (1961) "Foreword," in E. H. Sutherland, White Collar Crime (rev. ed.). New York: Holt, Rinehart & Winston.

CULLEN, F. T., B. G. LINK, and C. W. POLANZI (1982) "The seriousness of crime revisited: have attitudes toward white-collar crime changed?" Criminology 20 (May): 83-103.

CYERT, R. and J. MARCH (1963) A Behavioral Theory of the Firm. Englewood Cliffs, NJ: Prentice-Hall.

DEAL, T. E. and A. A. KENNEDY (1982) Corporate Cultures. Reading, MA: Addison-Wesley.

De MARE, G. (1976) Corporate Lives. New York: Van Nostrand.

DeMARIA, A. T., D. TARNOWIESKI, and R. GURMAN (1972) Manager Unions? AMA Research Report.

DILL, W. R., T. L. HILTON, and W. R. REITMAN (1962) The New Manager. Englewood Cliffs, NJ: Prentice-Hall.

DONALDSON, T. (1982) Corporations and Morality. Englewood Cliffs, NJ: Prentice-Hall.

DRUCKER, P. (1976) Management: Tasks, Responsibilities and Practices. New York: Harper & Row.

——— (1972) Concept of the Corporation (rev. ed.). New York: Monitor.

ERMANN, M. D. and R. J. LUNDMAN [eds.] (1978) Corporate and Governmental Deviance: Problems of Organizational Behavior in Contemporary Society. New York: Oxford University Press.

EVAN, W. M. (1976) Organization Theory: Structure, Systems, and Environments. New York: John Wiley.

EWING, D. (1977) "What business thinks about employee rights." Harvard Business Review 55 (September-October): 91-94.

FINNEY, H. C. and H. R. LESIEUR (1982) "A contingency theory of organizational crime," in S. B. Bacharach (ed.) Research in the Sociology of Organizations: A Research Annual. Greenwich, CT: JAI.

FISSE, B. (1981) "Community service as a sanction against corporations." Wisconsin Law Review, pp. 970-1017.

GALBRAITH, J. K. (1971) The New Industrial State (2nd ed.). New York: New American Library.

GEIS, G. (1973) "Deterring corporate crime," in R. Nader and M. Green (eds.) Corporate Power in America. New York: Grossman.

——— (1972) "Criminal penalties for corporate criminals." Criminal Law Bulletin (June): 377-392.

——— (1967) "White collar crime: the heavy electrical equipment antitrust cases of 1961," in M. B. Clinard and R. Quinney, Criminal Behavior Systems: A Typology. New York: Holt, Rinehart & Winston.

GOODMAN, W. (1963) All Honorable Men: Corruption and Compromise in American Life. Boston: Little, Brown.

GRAYMER, L. and F. THOMPSON [eds.] (1982) Reforming Social Regulation: Alternative Public Policy Strategies. Beverly Hills, CA: Sage.

GREEN, M. J. (1979) "The faked case against regulation." Washington Post (January 21).

GROSS, E. (1980) "Organization structure and organizational crime," pp. 52-77 in G. Geis and E. Stotland (eds.) White-Collar Crime: Theory and Research. Beverly Hills, CA: Sage.

——— (1978) "Organizational crime: a theoretical perspective," in N. Denzin (ed.) Studies in Symbolic Interaction. Greenwood, CT: JAI.

GRUMBLY, T. P. (1982) "Virtue revisited," pp. 93-119 in E. Bardach and R. A. Kagan (eds.) Social Regulation: Strategies for Reform. San Francisco: Institute for Contemporary Studies.

GUZZARDI, W., Jr. (1982) "Reagan's reluctant deregulators." Fortune, March 8, pp. 34-40.

HARTUNG, F. (1950/1977) "White-collar offenses in the wholesale meat industry in Detroit," in G. Geis and R. F. Meier (eds.) White-Collar Crime (rev. ed.). New York: Free Press.

HAY, G. and D. KELLEY (1974) "An empirical survey of pricefixing conspiracies." Journal of Law and Economics 17 (April): 13-39.

HERLING, J. (1962) The Great Price Conspiracy: The Story of the Antitrust Violations in the Electrical Industry. Washington, DC: Robert B. Luce.

HERMAN, E. S. (1981) Corporate Control, Corporate Power. New York: Cambridge University Press.

KAHN, A. E. (1982) "The political feasibility of regulatory reform: how did we do it?" in L. Graymer and F. Thompson (eds.) Reforming Social Regulation: Alternative Public Policy Strategies. Beverly Hills, CA: Sage.

KAHN, R. L., D. M. WOLFE, R. P. QUINN, J. D. SNOCK, and R. A. ROSENTHAL (1964) Organizational Stress. New York: John Wiley.

KAY, E. (1974) The Crisis in Middle Management. New York: Amacom.

KLEINFIELD, N. R. (1982) "The chief executive under stress." The New York Times, November 7, Sect. 3.

LANE, R. E. (1953/1977) "Why businessmen violate the law," pp. 102-117 in G. Geis and R. F. Meier (eds.) White-Collar Crime. New York: Free Press.

LEWIS, R. and R. STEWART (1961) The Managers: A New Examination of the English, German and American Executive. New York: New American Library.

LIPSETT, S. M. and W. SCHNEIDER (1978) "How's business? What the public thinks." Public Opinion (July/August): 41-47.

MADDEN, C. (1977) "Forces which influence ethical behavior," in C. Walton (ed.) The Ethics of Corporate Conduct. Englewood Cliffs, NJ: Prentice-Hall.

MARSHALL, J. and C. L. COOPER (1979) "Work experiences of middle and senior managers: the pressure and satisfactions." Management International Review 19: 81-96.

McKEAN, J. R. and R. J. MONSEN (1975) "Executive-compensation and the theory of the firm — an empirical study." Industrial Marketing Management 4 (June): 125-132.

MEIER, R. F. [ed.] (1977) Theory in Criminology: Contemporary Views. Beverly Hills, CA: Sage.

——— (1975) "Corporate crime as organizational behavior." Presented at the annual meetings of the American Society of Criminology, Toronto, October 30-November 2.

MORRIS, J. (1975) "Managerial stress and 'the cross of relationships,'" in D. Gowler and K. Legge (eds.) Managerial Stress. Epping: Gower Press.

MURRAY, T. J. (1973) "The revolt of the middle managers — phase two." Dun's 102 (August): 32-34.

NADER, R., M. J. GREEN, and J. SELIGMAN (1976) Taming the Giant Corporation. New York: Norton.

NEWMAN, D. (1958/1977) "White-collar crime," pp. 50-65 in G. Geis and R. F. Meier (eds.) White-Collar Crime. New York: Free Press.

——— (1953) "Public attitudes toward a form of white-collar crime." Social Problems 4 (January): 228-232.

OLINS, W. (1978) The Corporate Personality: An Inquiry into the Nature of Corporate Identity. New York: Mayflower.

PERROW, C. (1972) Complex Organizations: A Critical Essay. Chicago: Scott, Foresman.

PETERS, T.J. and R.H. WATERMAN, Jr. (1982) In Search of Excellence: Lessons from America's Best Run Corporations. New York: Harper & Row.

QUINNEY, R. (1964/1977) "The study of white-collar crime: toward a reorientation in theory and practice," pp. 283-296 in G. Geis and R.F. Meier (eds.) White-Collar Crime (rev. ed.). New York: Free Press.

——— (1963/1967) "Occupational structure and criminal behavior: prescription violation by retail pharmacists," in M.B. Clinard and R. Quinney, Criminal Behavior Systems: A Typology. New York: Holt, Rinehart & Winston.

REISS, A.J., Jr. (1978) "Organizational deviance," in M.D. Ermann and R.J. Lundman (eds.) Corporate and Governmental Deviance. New York: Oxford University Press.

RIEDEL, M. (1968) "Corporate crime and interfirm organization: a study of penalized Sherman Act violations." Graduate Sociology Club Journal 8: 74-97.

ROCKLEY, J.W. (1974) "The middle-management squeeze." Canadian Business Review 1: 37-40.

ROSS, I. (1980) "How lawless are big companies?" Fortune (December 1): 57-64.

ROWAN, R. (1981) Rekindling corporate loyalty." Fortune (February 9): 54-59.

SCHERER, F.M. (1980) Industrial Market Structure and Economic Performance (2nd ed.). Chicago: Rand McNally.

SHAPIRO, I.S. (1981) "Occupational health and safety," pp. 209-217 in T. Bradshaw and D. Vogel (eds.) Corporations and Their Critics: Issues and Answers to the Problems of Corporate Social Responsibilities. New York: McGraw-Hill.

SHAPIRO, K.P. (1981) "Improvements in attitudes of employees not spreading to many middle managers." Business Insurance 15: 26.

SHAPIRO, S. (1976) "A background paper on white collar crime." Presented at the Faculty Seminar on White Collar Crime, Yale Law School, February.

SHAPLEN, R. (1978) "Annals of crime: the Lockheed incident." The New Yorker, January 23, pp. 48-74; January 30, pp. 78-91.

SHERMAN, L.W. (1980) "A theoretical strategy for organizational deviance." Presented at the Conference on White-Collar and Economic Crime, International Sociological Association, Potsdam, New York, February.

SHORRIS, E. (1980) The Oppressed Middle: Politics of Middle Management, Scenes from Corporate Life. New York: Anchor/Doubleday.

SHOVER, N. (1978) "Defining organizational crime," in M.D. Ermann and R.J. Lundman (eds.) Corporate and Governmental Deviance: Problems of Organizational Behavior in Contemporary Society. New York: Oxford University Press.

SHRAGER, L.S. and J.F. SHORT, Jr. (1978) "Toward a sociology of organizational crime." Social Problems 25: 407-419.

SILK, L. and D. VOGEL (1976) Ethics & Profits: The Crisis of Confidence in American Business. New York: Simon & Schuster.

STAW, B.M. and E. SZWAJKOWSKI (1975) "The scarcity-munificence component of organizational environments and the commission of illegal acts." Administrative Science Quarterly 20 (September): 345-354.

STINCHCOMBE, A. L. (1965) "Social structure and organizations," pp. 142-193 in J. G. March (ed.) Handbook of Organizations. Chicago: Rand McNally.

STOKES, M. (1982) Conquering Government Regulations: A Business Guide. New York: McGraw-Hill.

STONE, C. (1975) Where the Law Ends: The Social Control of Corporate Behavior. New York: Harper & Row.

SUTHERLAND, E. H. (1949/1961) White Collar Crime (rev. ed.) New York: Holt, Rinehart & Winston.

——— (1945) "Is 'white-collar crime' crime?" American Sociological Review 10 (April): 132-139.

——— (1940) "White-collar criminality." American Sociological Review 5 (February): 1-12.

THACKRAY, J. (1981) "The new organization man." Management Today (September): 74-77, 168.

U.S. News & World Report (1982) "Corporate crime: the untold story." September 6, pp. 25-30.

VANDIVIER, K. (1972) "Why should my conscience bother me?" in R. L. Heinbroner (ed.) In the Name of Profit: Profiles of Corporate Irresponsibility. Garden City, NY: Doubleday.

VAUGHAN, E. (1982) "Toward understanding unlawful organizational behavior." Michigan Law Review 80 (June): 1377-1402.

——— (1981) "Recent developments in white-collar crime theory and research," in I. L. Barak-Glantz and R. Huff (eds.) The Mad, The Bad, and The Different. Lexington, MA: Lexington Books.

VOGEL, D. (1981) "Foreword," pp. vii-xv in T. Bradshaw and D. Vogel (eds.) Corporations and Their Critics: Issues and Answers to the Problems of Corporate Social Responsibilities. New York: McGraw-Hill.

WEAVER, P. (1978) "Regulation, social policy, and class conflict," pp. 193-219 in C. Argyris et al., Regulating Business: The Search for an Optimum. San Francisco: Institute for Contemporary Studies.

WHEELER, S. (1961) "Role conflict in correctional communities," pp. 229-259 in D. Cressey (ed.) The Prison: Studies of Institutional and Organizational Change. New York: Holt, Rinehart & Winston.

WILSON, J. Q. [Ed.] (1980) The Politics of Regulation. New York: Basic Books.

WOLFGANG, M. (1980) "Crime and punishment." New York Times, March 2, p. E-21.

——— (1979) "National survey of crime severity." University of Pennsylvania, mimeo.

WOODMANSEE, J. (1975) The World of a Giant Corporation: A Report from the GE Project. Seattle: North Country.

INDEX

Advertising, misrepresentations in,
15, 36, 79
Aerospace industry, 36, 56-57, 66-67,
83, 85, 115
government regulation and, 103, 104,
106, 109, 111, 125, 126
pressures in, 95-100 passim
violations in, 38, 46, 49, 58-59, 62, 64,
75, 76, 77, 120, 121, 148-149
Anti-trust violations. See Monopolies
Argyris, C., 150
Asch, P., 146
Atlantic Richfield Company, 152
Aubert, V., 11

Baldridge, Malcolm, 84
Bardach, E., 150, 155
Barnet, R., 139
Barnett, H. C., 153
Baumhart, R. C., 140
Block, M. K., 157
Board of directors, role of, 135-136
Bradshaw, T., 14, 152
Braithwaite, J., 10, 154-155, 158
Brenner, S. N., 140
Bribery. See Payoffs; Political
contributions, illegal
Building materials industry, 59, 73, 121
government regulation and, 106, 110,
117, 119, 128

Business equipment industry, 42, 55,
64, 69, 81, 82, 86
government regulation and, 104, 107,
109, 111, 116, 125
pressures in, 94, 101
violations in, 37, 56, 76, 78

Carroll, A. B., 139, 142
Chemical industry, 36-45 passim, 57-69
passim, 73, 80-81, 85-88 passim
government regulation and, 104, 106,
107, 110, 114, 116, 117, 118, 126, 127
pressures in, 93-100 passim
violations in, 47, 62, 64, 65, 75, 122,
124, 148
Clark, J. P., 133
Clinard, M. B., 11, 12, 15, 16, 17, 23, 40,
79, 84, 138, 139, 144-152 passim, 156
Competition, 53, 58-59, 107
and pricefixing, 120, 147
unfair practices in, 23, 61-65, 147-149
Consent orders, 158
Consolidated Edison of New York, 142
Consumer action, 12, 17, 80, 158
Consumer Product Safety Commission
(CPSC), 113, 151
Cooper, C. L., 140
Cooper, M. R., 141
Corporations
culture of, 23, 65, 70, 71, 133

ethics of. See Ethics, corporate
goals of, 17-18, 22-23, 145-146
impact of, 14, 16-17
internal auditing of, 41, 77
lines of communication in, 138-140
multinational, 14-15
public opinion of, 15-16, 19 n, 80
self-regulation of, 23, 47, 107-112,
151, 153-155
social responsibility of, 14, 15-16
social structure of, 14, 18, 131, 157
Cox, A., 141, 154, 163 n
Cressey, D. R., 11, 148
Crime
corporate, 14-19. See also Ethics,
corporate; Laws, corporate,
violations of
defined, 10
external factors in, 22, 144-155
internal factors in, 22, 53-70, 71-89,
95-100, 132-144, 148
as organizational behavior, 17-19
penalties for, 10-11
prevention of, 156-160
reporting of, 23, 114-129 passim
role of management in, 22-23, 47,
48, 71-89, 98, 132-144, 156-157
study of, 11-12, 17, 22
and violations of government
regulations, 47-50, 103-129 passim
occupational, 12-13
organizational, 12-19
white collar, 9-13
Cullen, F. T., 16
Customers, corporate fairness to, 15,
16, 41, 61, 62
Cyert, R., 145

Deal, T. E., 23
De Mare, G., 134
DeMaria, A. T., 141
Dill, W. R., 138
Donaldson, T., 125, 135, 162
Drucker, P., 21
Drug and cosmetics industry, 39, 40,
42, 79, 85, 89

government regulation and, 80, 103,
104, 154
violations in, 43, 57, 62, 99, 108, 114,
120, 148
DuPont de Nemours, E. I., &
Company, 152

Electric and appliance industry, 39, 68,
80-81, 86, 88-89
government regulation and, 44-45,
105, 106, 109, 110, 118, 119
pressures in, 60-61, 94, 97, 98, 101
violations in, 47, 56, 60-61, 63, 75, 143
Enforcement actions, 157-158. See also
Government regulation, effects of
Entertainment, improper, 36, 79
Environmental Protection Agency
(EPA), 18, 48, 61, 79, 113, 155
Equal Employment Opportunity
Commission (EEOC), 41, 61, 79, 113
Ethics, corporate, 16, 23, 35-51, 53-70
and competition, 53, 58-59, 61-65,
147-149
and corporate culture, 23, 65-70, 133
defined, 35
of executives' corporations, 39-47, 50
of executives' industries, 35-39, 50
and financial difficulties, 60-61,
144-146
and government regulation, 103-129
passim, 149-153
and history of corporation, 60, 65, 137
and law violations, 98, 107
and pressures on middle
management, 22-23, 95-102, 140-144
and size of community, 61, 66
and top management, 22-23, 41,
53-58, 65-89 passim, 132-140
and type of industry, 35-40, 50, 53,
59, 68, 147-149
Evan, W. M., 136
Ewing, D., 162
Executives. See Middle management;
Top management

Falsification of records, 15, 143-144

Federal Trade Commission (FTC), 18, 113

Financial difficulties as a factor in violations, 60-61, 144-146

Finney, H. C., 13, 14, 19 n

Fisse, B., 163 n

Folding carton conspiracy, 138-139, 149

Food and beverage industry, 45, 60-68 passim, 74, 77, 81-89 passim
government regulation and, 72, 105-109 passim, 118, 126, 127
pressures in, 93-97 passim, 100, 143-144
violations in, 46, 54-55, 57, 58, 64, 76, 100, 121, 123, 124, 143-144

Food and Drug Administration (FDA), 10, 113

Galbraith, J. K., 145

Geis, G., 143, 157, 158

General Electric Company, 143

General Motors Corporation, 161

Goodman, W., 148

Government regulation, 10, 23, 36, 41, 47-50, 98-99, 103-129, 149-153. See also Laws, corporate; names of individual agencies
agencies recommended for retention, 112-114; Table, 113
compliance with, 103, 114-124, 151, 157-158
consent orders, 158
criticisms of, 150, 152, 155
effects of, 50, 62, 78, 103, 105, 151, 156, 157-158
enforcement actions, 157-158
and corporate ethics, 103-129 passim, 149-153
middle management views on, 103-129, 151, 153, 155, 156
need for, 107-114, 149-153, 154, 156, 157
"politics" of, 153
support for, 150-152
types of, 149

Graymer, L., 150, 152, 155

Greed. See Competition

Green, M. J., 150

Gross, E., 13, 17, 133, 138

Grumbly, T. P., 154

Gulf Oil Corporation, 135-136

Guzzardi, W., Jr., 150

Hartung, F., 11

Hay, G., 148

Health care and supplies industry, 44, 48-49, 72, 81
government regulation and, 110, 117, 119
pressures in, 93, 98, 101

Heavy electric pricefixing conspiracy, 143

Herling, J., 143

Herman, E. S., 134-135, 135-136, 137, 142

H. J. Heinz Corporation, 143-144

Hollinger, R. C. 133

Industrial and farm equipment industry, 45, 48, 55, 60-69 passim, 73-74, 80, 82
government regulation and, 103, 108-111 passim, 119, 128
pressures in, 95, 96, 97, 100
violations in, 36, 37, 40, 49, 78, 121, 122, 123

Industrial espionage, 36, 161

Industries
represented in sample, 26; Table, 26. See also names of individual industries
self-regulation of, 107-112, 153-155. See also Corporations, self-regulation of

Industry associations, 111

Interstate Commerce Commission (ICC), 149

Issues studied, summary of, 22-23

Justice Department, 113

Kagan, R. A., 150, 155

Kahn, A. E., 140, 153
Kay, E., 141
Kelley, D., 148
Kennedy, A. A., 23
Kickbacks, 41, 61, 77, 79, 139
  reporting of, 114-115, 122-123
Kleinfield, N. R., 146

Lane, R. E., 11, 61, 146, 163 n
Law, corporate, 9, 10-11. See also
  Crime, corporate; Government
  regulation
  enforcement of, 156
  and ethics, 98, 107. See also Ethics
  protection for those reporting
  violations of, 125-129, 161-162
  violations of, 14-15, 18, 47-50, 53-70,
  74-79, 132-162 passim
    reporting, 114-129, 160-162
Lesieur, H. R., 13, 14, 19 n
Lewis, R., 138
Light industry, 123, 124, 127
Light machinery industry, 59, 61, 76
Lipset, S. M., 16
Lockheed Corporation, 149
Luce, C. F., 142

Madden, C., 134
Management. See Middle
  management; Top management
Manufacturing and marketing,
  comparative views of managers in,
  47, 62, 65, 71, 75, 79, 85, 95, 98, 103,
  114, 118, 120, 122, 125. See also names
  of specific industries
March, J.; 145
Marshall, J. C., 140
McKean, J. R., 84
Meier, R. F., 17
Metal industry, 85-86, 88
  ethics in, 44, 45, 54, 56, 63, 67, 68, 69,
  73, 74, 77, 80
  government regulation and, 104-116
  passim, 119, 120, 125, 127
  pressures in, 98, 101
  violations in, 47, 87, 121, 122, 123, 126,
  148

Middle management, 21-34, 131
  attitudes of, toward corporation,
  33-34, 39-47, 50
  decline of satisfaction in, 141
  interviews with, 29-34
    confidentiality of, 31, 32
    establishing trust in, 31-32, 33
    manner of conducting, 30-31
    questions in, 29-30
    schedules of, 29
    sources of financial support for, 33
  pressures on, 21, 91-102, 140-144
    in employee and management
    relations, 91, 140
    financial, 91, 140, 144
    and improper behavior, 22-23,
    95-100, 140, 142-144
    and individual ethics, 100-102, 142
    of job responsibilities, 140
    of lack of autonomy, 140, 141
    and personal life, 91-95
    quota, 91, 140
    table of, 92
    time, 91, 140
    types of, 91, 140
  relations with top management,
  21, 47, 72, 77, 91, 98-99, 139-144
  passim, 157, 159
  role of
    in corporate crime, 22-23, 98,
    142-144
    in corporation, 21, 131, 141
  sample of, interviewed, 24-29,
  165-175
    age of, 28
    characteristics of, 25-29, 131
    corporate distribution of, 25-26,
    171
    corporate size of, 26
    education of, 28-29
    industries represented in, 26;
    Table 26
    last position of, 27-28, 173-175
    length of retirement of, 28
    length of service of, 26-27
    locating, 24, 165-170

location of last position of, 27-28, 173-175
  methods of selection of, 24
  validity of, 25, 131
suggestions of, for control of violations, 156-162
types of executives in, 21
views of, on
  ethical differences among corporations, 53-70, 147; Tables, 54, 55
  government regulation, 103-129, 149-153, 155
  industries, 35-39, 50, 147-149
  industry self-regulation, 153-155
  legal violations, 47-50, 132-162 passim
  reporting violations, 114-129
  top management, 53-58, 71-89, 132-140, 156-157
Miller, R., 139
Molander, E. A., 140
Monopolies, 41, 50, 79, 149
Monsen, R. J., 84
Morris, J., 21
Motor vehicle industry, 85, 86-87, 89
  ethics of, 36, 39, 40, 42, 46-47, 57, 63, 67, 72
  government regulation and, 73, 82, 104, 108-109, 112, 116-122 passim, 127
  pressures in, 93-101 passim
  violations in, 48, 50, 59, 61, 64-65, 76, 77, 148

Nader, Ralph, 80, 149, 161
National Labor Relations Board (NLRB), 113
Newman, D., 11

Occupational Safety and Health Administration (OSHA), 18, 48, 50, 61, 113, 117, 151
Oil industry, 64, 72-73, 74, 85, 87, 88
  ethics of, 56, 67, 82
  government regulation and, 81, 106, 110, 119
  pressures in, 93, 95, 96, 98

violations in, 39, 43, 47, 50, 76-77, 121, 124, 126, 128
Olins, W., 23
Organizational behavior. See Crime, corporate, as organizational behavior
"Organizational deviance," 12

Paper industry, 43, 78, 100, 120, 122, 138-139, 147
Payoffs, 36, 41, 77
  foreign, 15, 36, 61, 79, 114-115, 123-124
  reporting of, 114-115, 123-124
Perks, 84
Peters, T. J., 23, 137, 163 n
Political contributions, illegal, 15, 41, 142
Pollution, 15, 149
Pressures. See Middle management, pressures on; Top management, pressures on
Prevention of corporate violations, 158-162
Pricefixing, 15, 36, 79, 147, 148
  management knowledge of, 138, 143
  reporting of, 114-115, 119-122

Quinney, R., 11, 12, 136

Rebates, illegal, 114-115, 122-123
Record industry, 37-38, 59, 62, 67, 96, 128
Regulatory agencies. See Government regulation; names of specific agencies
Reiss, A. J., 12, 17
Riedel, M., 148
Ross, I., 15

Safety
  product, 15, 41, 50, 79, 103, 149, 151
  worker, 15, 36, 41, 77, 79, 103, 149, 151, 152
    reporting violations of, 114, 117-119
Sample interviewed. See Middle management, sample of, interviewed
Savin Corporation, 84
Scherer, F. M., 18

Schneider, W., 16

Schrager, L. S., 17-18

Securities and Exchange Commission (SEC), 113, 114, 139, 144, 150, 156

Seneca, J. J., 146

Shapiro, Irving, 152

Shapiro, S., 17

Shaplen, R., 149

Sherman, L. W., 17

Shorris, E., 21

Short, J. F., Jr., 17-18

Shover, N., 17

Silk, L., 34 n, 83, 131, 146, 152, 155, 160

Soap industry, 37, 43, 48, 55-56, 72, 105

Social control of corporate violations, 156-162

Sporkin, Stanley, 156

Staw, B. M., 146

Stewart, R., 138

Stinchcombe, A. L., 147

Stokes, M., 152

Stone, C., 23, 139, 142

Sutherland, Edwin H., 10-11, 17, 148

Szwajkowski, E., 146

Taxes, 15, 79, 85

Thompson, F., 150, 152, 155

Tire industry, 59, 60, 63, 66, 69, 74
  government regulation and, 38, 43-44, 82, 109, 110-111, 112, 117, 122, 126, 128
  pressures in, 93, 96, 101
  violations in, 46, 76

Top management, 18, 161-162
  compensation of, 83-89
  and corporate culture, 68-69, 133, 136
  and corporate ethics, 41, 53-58, 65-66, 67-68, 89, 107, 132-140, 145, 146
  and middle management. See Middle management, relations with top

management; Middle management, views of, on top management mobility of, 136-137
  personal ambition of, 56-58, 133, 136-137, 145
  personal problems of, 135
  pressures on, 135, 146
  relations with board of directors, 135-136
  types of executives in, 136-140
  views of, on employee rights, 161-162
  and violations
    knowledge of, 74-79, 89, 138-139, 143-144, 156
    responsibility for condemning, 79-83, 89, 120, 122, 123, 159-160
    role of, in, 22-23, 47, 48, 71-89, 98, 132-144, 156-157

Tylenol deaths, 154

Vandivier, K., 161

Vaughan, E., 11, 12, 14, 137, 147

Violations. See Laws, corporate, violations of; Crime, corporate; Ethics, corporate

Vogel, D., 14, 34 n, 83, 131, 146, 152, 153, 155, 160

Waterman, R. H., 23, 137, 163 n

Weaver, P., 153

Westinghouse Electric Corporation, 143

Wheeler, S., 102

Wilson, J. Q., 150, 153

Wolfgang, M., 16

Woodmansee, J., 143

Yeager, P. C., 15, 16, 17, 23, 79, 84, 138, 139, 144-152 passim, 156

ABOUT THE AUTHOR

MARSHALL B. CLINARD is one of the leading figures in the study of corporate and other white collar crime. An Emeritus Professor of Sociology from the University of Wisconsin, where he taught for 35 years, he previously taught on the faculty of the University of Iowa and Vanderbilt University. He has also served as Chief of Criminal Statistics, U.S. Bureau of the Census, Chief of Analysis and Reports of the wartime Office of Price Administration, and as a consultant on crime and urban development in India and other countries. In 1971 he was awarded the prestigious Edwin H. Sutherland Award for Distinguished Contributions to Criminology of the American Society of Criminology. He has been President of the Society for the Study of Social Problems and the Midwest Sociological Society. This is the tenth book of which he was the author or editor. These include a classic study entitled *The Black Market* (1952), a landmark piece in the field of illegal business behavior; *Corporate Crime* (1979, with Peter C. Yeager); and several textbooks, including *Sociology of Deviant Behavior* (5th edition, 1979). Many of his articles have focused on white collar and corporate crime, while others have touched on such topics as comparative criminology, crime in developing countries, community development and slums, and deviant behavior. He now resides in Santa Fe, New Mexico, where he is a Distinguished Research Professor in Sociology at the University of New Mexico.